# A Primer in Augustinian Spirituality

I0834712

A Primer in

# Augustinian Spirituality

## Communion, Participation, Mission

Joseph T. Kelley

In Memoriam
Kevin W. Salemme
*Frater Cordis Nostri*

*Cito de terra abstulisti vitam eius*
*et securior eum recordor*
—Saint Augustine, *Confessions*

Published in the United States by New City Press
136 Madison Avenue, Floors 5 & 6, PMB #4290
New York, NY 10016
www.newcitypress.com

©2026 Joseph T. Kelley

Cover design and layout by Miguel Tejerina
Cover photo: Anthony Aneese Totah Jr (edited)

Library of Congress Cataloging-in-Publication Data
Library of Congress Control Number: 2026931622
ISBN: 978-1-56548-740-6 (paper)
ISBN: 978-1-56548-741-3 (e-book)

Printed in the United States of America

# Contents

# Foreword

When an author is not only knowledgeable but also finds it enjoyable to write about a particular topic, it is immediately evident in the style, content and creation of the finished product. In this book, *A Primer in Augustinian Spirituality: Communion, Participation, Mission*, Joseph Kelley invites us into his vast knowledge of Saint Augustine and the Augustinian tradition. At the same time, he shares with us the joy that exploring Augustinian Spirituality brings to his heart.

From the beginning pages of this book, we are welcomed into the world of Saint Augustine of Hippo and introduced to the spirituality that emerged from his life and writings, and that has endured throughout the centuries. As readers, we are invited to explore some of the most important themes in the life of Aurelius Augustinus. Kelley highlights the spirituality that grew from Augustine's restless search for fulfillment, preserved for us in his *Confessions* and developed in his preaching, letters and many books. From Augustine's fourth to fifth-century ministry as bishop of the ancient port city of Hippo in North Africa, Kelley then traces the early development of the Order of Saint Augustine in the middle of the thirteenth century in Italy, and shows how the Augustinian tradition continues to attract, inspire and assist people around the globe today.

Joseph Kelley has many years of experience of research, teaching, and writing in his academic career of over five decades at Merrimack College in North Andover, Massachusetts (USA). He offers a unique viewpoint informed by his direct participation in organizing and implementing a *Pellegrinaggio* (Pilgrimage) that follows the footsteps of Augustine along a path of conversion which culminated in a garden in northern Italy. Kelley's distinctive perspective has also been shaped by his many years of involvement in various academic symposia in North Africa, and enriched by his love for all things "Augustine." He brings the fifth-century Bishop of Hippo alive in such a way that the modern reader, student, searcher, and pilgrim can find points of relevance today.

The title of this book indicates that this is a *Primer*, written to introduce the reader to the fundamentals of Augustinian Spirituality. Dr. Kelley structures the book using the three-fold process of the synodal way, which the universal Catholic Church has been developing over the past few years. The themes of *Communion, Participation* and *Mission* assist the reader to explore in a thematic way some of the most important aspects of Augustinian Spirituality.

In the first part of this book, *Communion*, our author begins with the central focus of Augustinian Spirituality, and in fact any Christian Spirituality, Jesus Christ. Augustinian Spirituality is Christocentric and so the first three chapters of this book present us with some of the most relevant aspects of Augustine's relationship with Christ. Pope Leo XIV's motto *In Illo uno unum* recalls the words of Saint Augustine, which he preached on the *Exposition on Psalm 127*, insisting that "in the one Christ we are one." For Augustine, Christ is what unites us into true communion with God and one another. The incarnate Word was the One to ignite Augustine's heart in the process of his call to conversion from darkness to light, from the search to satisfy his own desires to putting on the Lord Jesus Christ, and finding true fulfillment in living in communion with Christ and with others on the common pilgrimage on his way to God.

In the second part, *Participation*, each theme presented could be treated in a separate book. In the past few years, there has been so much discussion, research and writing about Artificial Intelligence, in short, AI. It is a reality which touches and influences all aspects of what it means to be human. In the Augustinian world, we like to offer an alternative meaning to AI, and invite those with whom we share our common pilgrimage to think of AI not as Artificial Intelligence, but rather as Augustinian Interiority. Christ is the center of Augustinian Spirituality. The work of going within and exploring the interior sacred space of each person is the way and the goal of discovering Christ. This *Primer* explores the themes of Listening, Memory, Interiority as the building blocks of entering within to discover God. It is from the sacred space within where one is able to truly know oneself and therefore truly know God. From the resulting discoveries of the journey within we can then discover how we participate as the Body of Christ through Friendship, Hospitality and Forgiveness. Augustinian Spirituality is both interior and social, and so these themes become critical parts of the framework in building the external structure of an Augustinian spiritual journey. The final section of *Participation* unfolds by encouraging the reader to embrace Humility, Poverty and Peace as sacred gifts that enlighten the journey from the interior exploration of Christ's mystical presence within, to the external graces and virtues expressed in the relationships we develop with our brothers and sisters.

The final part of this *Primer* develops the third synodal theme of *Mission*. Although Mission also includes all of the previously developed themes in this book, the theme of Hope offers a fitting conclusion to this thoughtfully developed structure. Hope, which "does not disappoint" (Romans 5:5), is one of the critical themes for Augustine's ministry as Bishop of Hippo and theologian. It is the bedrock upon which rest all the other themes of Augustinian Spirituality that help construct a vibrant way of living out one's relationship with Christ and with the world in concrete ways. In reality, the theme of Hope is present throughout each part of this *Primer* but deserves special mention and finds its proper place as the concluding section.

One of the early stages of initial formation as an Augustinian is called the Novitiate. It is a complete calendar year dedicated to discernment, prayer and discovery of Augustine, the vowed life, the history of the Order, and Augustinian Spirituality. The person living that stage of formation is rightly called a Novice. For those who are attracted to this book because it is a *Primer*, I believe that the style, structure and content which Dr. Kelley selected will offer you as a "novice" in Augustinian Spirituality the correct tools and vocabulary to ignite a spark within, which will encourage further research and discovery. For those who are more seasoned pilgrims on the path of Augustinian Spirituality, you will find a succinct and fulfilling refresher, which will nourish both your mind and heart on your journey toward God.

For Augustine, God is "ever ancient and ever new." There is no time, no moment which can hold God captive. There is always something new in the God who always is. So, too, with Augustinian Spirituality. The themes presented in this *Primer* are not "new" in the sense that they are recently discovered. Rather, the themes presented here are even more ancient than the protagonist whose name is attached to the spirituality that they represent. However ancient they may be, these themes are also new in two ways. They are new in the way they touched the life of a fourth and fifth-century man on his restless search for God. And they come alive in new ways when the modern reader is invited to apply these themes to the lived reality which he or she experiences each day.

As you explore the following pages, imagine yourself on a pilgrimage with each theme representing a signpost giving you direction on which way to proceed. I encourage you to spend some time allowing each of the signs along the way to take root within so that they become useful tools to aid you along the journey. May every theme presented in the sections on *Communion, Participation* and *Mission* inspire you to explore more intimately a spirituality that will lead you further along the path to self-discovery and your relationship with God. You do not necessarily have to follow the order presented in this *Primer*. You can begin by finding one that speaks most to you and after exploring all that theme has to offer, allow your discovery to point you to the next step along the journey. Allow the themes to speak to your heart and you will be surprised by what they have to offer.

Very Rev. Joseph L. Farrell, OSA
Prior General
Order of Saint Augustine

# Preface

My first Augustinian memory is of a priest who regularly came to our parish for Sunday Mass. I was only about eight or nine years old at the time, but I remember how his sermons held the congregation's interest. After Mass, people would discuss what he had said. My dad told me that he was such a good preacher because he was an Augustinian, a teacher at Villanova University, which was just a few miles away. I later learned he was Father Robert Sullivan, OSA, Dean of Arts and Sciences. I don't remember anything he said, of course. But the effect he had, so many years ago, on the people of Saint Monica Parish in Berwyn, Pennsylvania, has stayed with me ever since.

Eventually, I was fortunate enough to study with teachers like Father Sullivan, first at Augustinian Academy in New York City, and then at Villanova University. I joined the Order of Saint Augustine and lived in community as a friar for fourteen years, years I still cherish for the spiritual formation and lifelong friendships they provided. For fifty years, I was privileged to teach theology at Merrimack College, an Augustinian College in Massachusetts. Little did I realize, as a child who observed Father Sullivan from a distance, that I would so closely follow his Augustinian path.

Now, as a husband, father, grandfather, and lay affiliate of the Augustinians, the writings of Saint Augustine of Hippo continue to enrich my own faith and help me navigate the challenges of life. As a student of his thought, I have introduced Augustine to hundreds of my own students. In this little volume, I introduce you to him, or, more accurately, I introduce you to my understanding of his spirituality.

During my last ten years at Merrimack College, I taught in the graduate programs of spirituality and spiritual direction. Our students, most of whom were transitioning to second careers related to spirituality, came from a vast variety of religious affiliations, professional backgrounds, and points of view. One thing they all had in common was a desire to understand what spirituality is and how it relates to people's lives in today's world. They represented a wide spectrum of faith and experience, from Cameroonian Catholic priests to American Unitarian women. Many were religiously affiliated; some were not. But they all shared what Augustine called a restless heart seeking to probe the mysteries of life and the soul. They often came to mind as I was writing this book.

Presenting the thought of someone as prolific and insightful as Saint Augustine is a formidable task. The limitations of my own perspective and experience are all too evident to me. To background my own thinking, and foreground Augustine himself, I quote him prodigiously. As far as possible in an introductory book like this, the words of such an influential writer, rhetorician, and saint should be allowed to speak for themselves, even as we seek to understand and interpret them. At the end of this preface, there is a list of abbreviations for the titles of Augustine's works that I cite throughout the book.

One of the great resources for English-speaking Augustine scholars is *The Works of Saint Augustine: A Translation for the 21st Century*, published by New City Press, a division of Focolare Media, in collaboration with the Augustinian Heritage Institute. Almost all of the citations from Augustine in this book are from that translation. I am also indebted to the Italian Province of the Augustinians for easy access to Augustine's Latin text at www.augustinus.it.

The excellent book by Bishop Luis Marin de San Martin, OSA, *The Augustinians: Origins and Spirituality*, brings together much of the recent scholarship on the Augustinians and their spirituality (Institutum Historicum Augustinianum, 2012). I recommend it for those who wish to delve further into this topic. I also recommend the newly published book by Father Arthur Purcaro, OSA, *Building a Better World: A Contemporary Augustinian Perspective* (Focolare Media, New City Press, 2025). He applies the spirit and counsels of Augustine's *Monastic Rule* to integral environmentalism and extends Augustinian spirituality into the pursuit of justice and peace.

I wish to thank the many collaborators whose keen insights, corrections, conversations, and suggestions have enriched this text immensely. They include Gary Brandl, at New City Press, a longtime associate and superb editor; Augustinian friars from different countries, including Ifeanyi Hilary Basil, Antonio Carrón de la Torre, Andrew Batayola, Kevin DePrinzio, Raymond Dlugos, Allan Fitzgerald, Bitrus Galadima, Bryan Kerns, Daniel Madden, Gary McCloskey, Blair Nuyda, Jude Ossai, Ian Wilson, and Philip Yang; Augustinian Sister Sara Cozzolongo, from the monastery of San Salvatore at Lecceto, Italy; and Augustinian laity from across the world, including Vicki Blaszak, Mary Burke, Catherine Conybeare, Maureen Cunningham, Judith Duncan, Adrienne Franciosi, Trish Gannon, Timothy Hart, Edward and Kathy Hastings, and Mary McCormick. I am grateful to the Rev. James Ennis for his valuable Evangelical Christian perspective, and to my friend, Dr. Yehezkel Landau, whose devotion to and leadership in interreligious and inter-spiritual dialogue is a constant inspiration. Finally, I heartily thank Father Joseph Farrell, OSA, for his encouragement, wisdom, and friendship of many years.

# Abbreviations of Works Cited

|  |  |
|---|---|
| *Against Lying: To Consentius* | *Ag Lying Con* |
| *Answer to Faustus, a Manichean* | *Ans Faus* |
| *Argument with the Skeptics* | *Arg Skps* |
| *City of God* | *CG* |
| *A Commentary on the Epistle to the Galatians* | *Com Ep Gal* |
| *Confessions* | *Conf* |
| *Exposition of the Psalms* | *Ex Ps* |
| *The Grace of Christ and Original Sin* | *Gr Chr Org Sin* |
| *Homilies on the Gospel of John* | *Hom Gos Jn* |
| *Homilies on the First Epistle of John* | *Hom 1 Jn* |
| *Instructing Beginners in Faith* | *Instr Bg* |
| *Letter* | *L* |
| *The Life of Saint Augustine,* by Saint Possidius | *Life* |
| *Miscellany of Questions in Response to Simplician* | *Misc Smp* |
| *Miscellany of Eighty-Three Questions* | *Misc 83* |
| *Monastic Rule* | *Rule* |
| *Nature and Grace* | *Nat Gr* |
| *On Order* | *Ord* |
| *The Punishment and Forgiveness of Sins and the Baptism of Little Ones* | *Forg Sins Bap Lit* |
| *Questions on the Gospels* | *Ques Gosp* |
| *Questions on the Heptateuch* | *Ques Hep* |
| *Revisions* | *Revisions* |
| *Sermon* | *S* |
| *Sermon to the People of the Church of Caesarea* | *S Ch Caes* |
| *Soliloquies* | *Sol* |
| *The Teacher* | *Tchr* |
| *Teaching Christianity* | *Tchg Ch* |
| *The Trinity* | *Trin* |
| *True Religion* | *Tr Rel* |
| *The Work of Monks* | *Wk Monks* |
| *Unfinished Work in Answer to Julian* | *Ans Jul* |

# Introduction

Many spiritual traditions have enriched the Catholic Church over the centuries. One of the oldest is Augustinian spirituality. It emerged early in the history of the Church, in the life and writings of Saint Augustine of Hippo (354–430). In his *Confessions*, Augustine famously shared the struggles and questions, the doubts and difficulties that pervaded the long process of his conversion to Christ. In a very real sense, Augustinian spirituality was conceived in Augustine's restless heart and birthed during his journey toward faith. It developed and matured as Augustine continued to reflect on his faith in Christ and on the nature of the Church, which he served as priest and bishop for forty years.

Augustine would not have distinguished among what we identify today as the separate but related disciplines of spirituality, theology, and philosophy. Rather, he spoke and wrote about philosophy as the "love of wisdom" (from the two Greek words *philia* and *sophia*). He thought of himself as a "Christian philosopher." Like other ancient Greek and Roman philosophers, his quest was not limited to intellectual abstraction. It was a search for wisdom that promised happiness and fulfillment, and a program for how to live one's life. When reading Augustine's many writings, we find spirituality, philosophy, and theology intermingled, enriching and defining each other in this pursuit of wisdom.

Ultimately, Augustine's restless heart found this wisdom in Christ, the Incarnation and revelation of God's love for humankind. It was in the light of divine love that Augustine read Sacred Scripture, taught Christian doctrine, and led liturgical worship. For Augustine, then, the source and summit of spiritual life is the mystery of divine love, a mystery discovered in the depths of the soul and shared in communion with others.

## Life of Saint Augustine

Aurelius Augustinus was born on November 13, 354, in North Africa. His town was called Thagaste, today the modern city of Souk Ahras, in Algeria. In those years, it was at the southern edge of the Roman Empire, far from the centers of power and influence. Monica, his mother, was a devout Christian of indigenous Berber ethnicity. Patricius, his father, was a mid-level Roman official who converted to Christianity only at the end of his life. Augustine had at least one brother and one sister that we know of.

The family spoke Latin and perhaps were familiar with the local Berber dialect. However, they identified as Romans. Monica and Patricius recognized the intelligence of their son and wanted him to achieve success in the Roman fashion by training to become a rhetorician. Knowing how to speak effectively, how to sway audiences and influence people, was the way to achieve status and power, and maybe to escape the remote outback of Africa.

His parents saved and borrowed money for Augustine's education. At age seventeen, he left home to study in the great city of Carthage, in what is today Tunisia. He excelled in his studies. However, it was a tumultuous time personally. The young Augustine met and moved in with a girlfriend. They soon had a son whom they named Adeodatus (gift of God). He also joined the Manichean sect, a curious mix of Persian, Jewish, and Christian religions. At some point during these same years, his father died. When he returned home to Thagaste, with companion and son in tow, bragging about his newfound religion, his recently widowed mother, Monica, was not amused. At first, she refused to let him in the house. Eventually, fondness for her bright, ambitious, but charming son gained him entry. She resolutely continued to pray that he would become a Catholic Christian.

After a year or so, Augustine returned to Carthage, this time to teach. Then, when he was about twenty-nine, he left Carthage for Rome, where the students were supposedly more serious and of a higher quality. Having spent an unprofitable year in Rome, he won the post of rhetorician in the imperial court, which in those years was in the northern Italian city of Milan. He had realized his parents' dream. At the age of thirty, he held one of the most influential posts in the Empire. But he was not happy. His public duties, along with his teaching, weighed heavily on him.

Monica eventually joined her son in Milan. She pressured him to send his longtime female companion back to Africa and arranged a proper marriage to a wealthy but very young Milanese heiress. In the midst of this personal turmoil and professional anxiety, Augustine met Ambrose, the Catholic bishop of Milan. Under Ambrose's influence, Augustine began to reconsider the Bible, which he had previously rejected as inferior literature. He was also introduced to the community of learned Christian philosophers in that city. In their company, he started to read what is called Neoplatonic philosophy and discovered its emphasis on interiority. In the spring of 386, he had a profound experience of divine grace while reading Saint Paul's Letter to the Romans and decided to be baptized. Together with his son, Adeodatus, and his good friend Alypius, Augustine was baptized in Milan in April of 387. He was thirty-two.

Augustine chose to forgo marriage, to resign his position, and to return to Africa in order to live a life of prayer and study. Monica died and was buried in the Roman port city of Ostia on their return journey. Eventually, Augustine arrived home in Thagaste, where he established a community of like-minded Christian friends. But more changes awaited him. His beloved son, Adeodatus, died not long after they had returned. A few years later, during a visit to the coastal city of Hippo, today Annaba in Algeria, Augustine was recognized as the famous rhetorician who had become a Christian. The people "seized him" during Mass, as he would later write, and presented him to the bishop for ordination. He had to give up his dream of a quiet community life in Thagaste.

By 395, Augustine was bishop of Hippo, where he served the Church until his death on August 28, 430. During his years of ministry, he was a prodigious writer. We have almost four hundred of his sermons and three hundred letters to a great variety of people, as well as over two hundred books, including the classic texts *Confessions*, *City of God*, *Trinity*, and *Teaching Christianity*.

He left us five million words in all, more than any ancient author. From these works, his spirituality emerges with insights into human meaning and purpose, in the light of God's love.

## The Origins of Augustinian Spirituality

In the months before his conversion, in one of the many conversations about God and faith that he had with his friends, Augustine learned about an earlier Christian spiritual movement that had begun in the late 200s. In their hunger for a deeper spiritual life, many third and early fourth-century Christians withdrew from the world to dwell in remote regions of Egypt, Syria, and the Holy Land. Leaving society behind, they sought to lead lives of intense prayer and sacrifice in the wilderness. Augustine marveled at the conviction and dedication of fervent souls such as Antony of Egypt, a leader of this movement. Upon hearing the Gospel of Matthew, Antony took the words to be addressed to himself. "Go and sell all you possess and give the money to the poor: you will have treasure in heaven. Then come, follow me" (Matthew 19:21; *Confessions* VIII.12.29).

The story of Antony's life had a profound effect on Augustine as he struggled with his own decision to become a Christian. It stirred a spiritual fervor in his own soul and turned his always passionate nature to the possibility of a life infused by the Spirit of God. Ultimately, it inspired him not only to request Baptism but also to seek a spiritual path similar to Antony's. He, too, wanted to forsake all and follow Christ, to devote his life to prayer and contemplation in imitation of the holy hermits who had joined Antony in Egypt.

However, Augustine did not choose the desert as the locus for his spiritual life. When he arrived home, instead of withdrawing into African wastelands, Augustine founded a community that gathered around the garden, the open, peaceful enclosure around which houses in the late Roman Empire were built. Over the years, communities inspired by Augustine's example became centers of spirituality and contemplation, new gardens of Eden redeemed by Christ and peopled by Christians, living out their faith amidst the busy population centers in Roman North Africa.

His vision of committed Christian men and women, lay and ordained, living in simple houses of prayer among the People of God, inspired a new kind of Christian spirituality. It combined the contemplation of the desert with an active ministry in town or city. It integrated spirituality with service, contemplation with community, and humility with hospitality for all who sought God. Even after he was called to be priest and then bishop in the busy port city of Hippo, Augustine himself continued to live in prayerful community and shared poverty with his fellow clerics.

These new communities sought Augustine's counsel and guidance as they strove to live out the Gospel. His response to their request came to be known as his *Monastic Rule*. It is a relatively short document of eight brief chapters that emphasizes love of God and love of one another, and calls for imitation of the first Christians, as described in the Acts of the Apostles. "All the believers were one in heart and mind. No one claimed that any of their possessions was their own, but they shared everything they had" (Acts 4:32).

Augustinian spirituality thus germinated during the process of Augustine's conversion to Christ. It matured in his desire to live out his Christian faith in a community of believers, living together in harmony, "intent upon God" (*Rule* 1.2). It spread roots and bore fruit during Augustine's forty years of service to the Church as priest and bishop. In his many books, sermons, and letters, Augustine explored and elaborated the nature of Christian life and the spirituality it engendered. Sixteen hundred years later, his spiritual insights continue to inspire men and women in countries and cultures across the globe.

## The Augustinian Tradition

After Augustine's death, his example and writings continued to guide small monastic communities of men and women. However, the troubled political history of North Africa slowly suppressed Christian communities and institutions in that region. Monasteries that followed Augustine's *Rule* and embraced his vision of the spiritual life either closed or migrated north across the Mediterranean. Soon, groups of lay people and clerics in Europe found inspiration and direction in Augustine's *Monastic Rule* for new monastic foundations. His *Rule* was also adopted in many places across Europe by priests who chose to live a more intense spiritual life in community with their bishop. These diocesan communities became known as Augustinian Canons. Augustine's *Rule* was the "canon" or statute that ordered their life together and inspired their common prayer.

There was a significant spiritual movement across Europe during the thirteenth and fourteenth centuries. The political and economic life of the continent developed at a rapid pace in these years. Urbanization and social change left thousands of people seeking a deeper spiritual life, beyond routine religious belief and customary observance. Francis of Assisi, in the Italian region of Umbria, is perhaps the most famous of these hermits who left everything and inspired others to follow the Gospel and join him in a life of evangelical poverty.

West of Umbria, in the region of Tuscany, there were also many hermit communities that gathered adjacent to the new burgeoning towns and cities in central Italy. In 1244, Pope Innocent IV organized these Tuscan hermits into a new mendicant order and gave them the *Rule of Saint Augustine* to follow. Thus, the Order of Saint Augustine was born. It expanded significantly in 1256, in what was called the Grand Union with other communities of hermits across Italy and Europe. The new order of mendicant friars fashioned itself according to Augustine's original vision, combining contemplation with ministry, spirituality with service, prayer with community, and simplicity of life with hospitality for others. The *Constitutions of the Order of Saint Augustine* state, "Our Order from its very beginning has recognized Saint Augustine as its father, master, and spiritual guide, not only because it has received the Rule and the name of the Order from him, but also because it has received from him its doctrine and spirituality" (*Constitutions* I.1.2).

The Order grew quickly. Augustinian friars became preachers of the Gospel, university professors, spiritual directors, and guides. Their various ministries provided a whole new impetus for the spread of Augustinian spirituality. The early saints of the Order, such as Nicholas of Tolentine, Clare of Montefalco, Rita of Cascia, and Thomas of Villanova, among many others, became exemplars of that spirituality.

Today, the Order of Saint Augustine, both the friars and contemplative nuns, along with the men and women of the Augustinian Recollects, the Augustinians of the Assumption, the Discalced Augustinians, as well as the many other religious congregations that follow the Rule of Saint Augustine, are the contemporary guardians and emissaries of Augustinian spirituality. The wider Augustinian family includes many lay people associated with one of the Augustinian orders in different ways. There are multiple lay fraternities, societies, and Third Order Augustinians who continue to find in Augustine inspiration for their spiritual lives.

## The Reception and Renewal of Augustinian Spirituality

Across the centuries, different generations of Christians have read and received Augustine's thought differently, influenced by the perspectives and problems of their own time and place. That has left us with many different readings of his ideas. As we have seen, during the so-called Dark Ages of Europe, it was his *Monastic Rule* that influenced European monasticism, along with *Confessions* and *Teaching Christianity* that remained perennial favorites for devout Christians seeking to live a spiritual life. Centuries later, the intensive philosophical and theological debates at the medieval universities in Europe favored a more doctrinal and apologetic reading of his philosophy and theology, sometimes eclipsing the spirituality at the heart of his faith.

By contrast, the Renaissance discovered a more humane Augustine. The fourteenth-century Italian poet Francesco Petrarch found a rich source of Christian humanism in Augustine's appreciation of classical Greek and Roman culture. What we might call Petrarch's humanistic spirituality drew from his intense reading of *Confessions* and a deep appreciation of Augustine's keen psychological insights. Petrarch regularly carried a small "pocket edition" of *Confessions* with him, a gift from his confessor, the Italian Augustinian friar Denis de Borgo San Sepolcro. Unlike medieval hierarchs and professors, however, Petrarch was not much interested in Christian apologetics.

Two centuries later, the German Augustinian Martin Luther once again brought Augustine's theology to the fore. On a personal level, Luther found much comfort and guidance for his troubled conscience in Augustine's understanding of divine grace. He avidly studied Augustine's interpretation of Saint Paul, which highlighted the primacy of grace for the spiritual life of a Christian. Luther, of course, preached and wrote about reform in the Church and was a leading figure in the Protestant Reformation. However, given the ecclesial and political situation of his time, as well as his own personal theological proclivities, Luther did not address many Augustinian themes such as interiority, contemplation, and sanctification.

After the Reformation, the sixteenth to seventeenth-century Dutch bishop, Cornelius Jansen, espoused a Catholic version of Augustine's theology of grace. Jansen actively opposed the French Jesuits' emphasis on free will, which he thought obscured the need for God's grace. It was a passionate theological debate with profound implications for the spiritual lives of untold numbers of Catholics. The Abbey of Port-Royale, outside Paris, promoted a severe reading of Jansen's interpretation of Augustine. This influenced the education of thousands of French clergy and Irish clergy who studied in France, since Protestant England prohibited Catholic seminaries in Ireland. Generations of these priests educated in a rather dour Augustinianism spread their particular understanding of Catholic spirituality across France, Ireland, French Canada, and America. It left Catholics in these regions with a spirituality devoid of the empathetic humanism that Petrarch had so admired in Augustine.

In the nineteenth and twentieth centuries, there was a resurgence of interest in Patristics, which is the study of the Fathers of the Church, that is, the influential bishops, priests, and theologians of the first six centuries of Christianity. This renewed interest in Patristics attracted attention to the wider corpus of Augustine's writings and encouraged new consideration of his thought in its proper historical context. Scholars began to study the writings of Augustine that had been ignored by previous generations. There was renewed interest in his *Sermons* and *Letters*, his *Expositions of the Psalms*, his *Homilies on the Gospel of John*, and *Homilies on the First Epistle of John*. As a result, dimensions of his thought expressed in these writings have received much more attention in recent decades. What has emerged is a new appreciation of Augustine's own spiritual life, of his interpretations of Scripture, and of his relationship with Christ. This research has also surfaced the spiritual guidance and pastoral care he offered his people.

The Second Vatican Council (1962–1965) encouraged all religious orders to revisit and revive their founders' spirit as they responded to the social conditions of the times (*Decree on the Adaptation and Renewal of Religious Life*, no. 2). In light of this call, the Augustinians engaged the advances in Augustinian studies to enrich their spiritual lives and to share a newfound appreciation of Augustinian spirituality with the wider Augustinian family of lay people.

## Augustinian Spirituality Today

This volume draws from the revitalization of Augustinian thought since the Second Vatican Council. My approach also takes courage from the Council's call for continuing dialogue with "the joys and the hopes, the griefs and the anxieties" of the "whole of humanity" (*Pastoral Constitution on the Church in the Modern World: Joy and Hope* nos. 1, 2). The assumption in these pages is that Augustinian spirituality uniquely addresses our "place and role in the universe, the meaning of our individual and collective strivings, and the ultimate destiny of reality and of humanity" (no. 3). In that spirit, the book takes three approaches to the topic, three ways of organizing the immense breadth and depth of Augustine's spirituality and its development in the Augustinian tradition: communion, participation, mission.

*Communion* is the heart of Augustinian spirituality, an interior life lived in mystical union with God and communion with others. Chapter one investigates how the restless human heart discovers and receives the revelation of divine love in Christ. Chapter two explores conversion as surrender to and sacrifice with Christ. Chapter three presents Augustine's understanding of Church as the Body of Christ, and as shared contemplation of the mystery of union with God and with each other in Christ.

*Participation* looks at practice, at the personal and communal dynamics that comprise Augustinian spiritual life on a daily basis. These include three triads: listening, interiority, and memory, in chapter four; friendship, hospitality, and forgiveness, in chapter five; and humility, poverty, and peace, in chapter six. These nine practices incorporate the interior mystery of communion with Christ with the habits of daily life.

Part three presents the theme of *Mission*. Chapter seven explores what Augustinian spirituality offers to the wider Church, to other religions, and to those who do not subscribe to any religion. It proposes that Augustine's insights into the human condition and his faith in God's love for humanity inspire hope for our shared future.

Because of the experience, vision, and perspective of its originator, Augustinian spirituality has a universalism about it, a passionate urgency that enriches Christians and others who seek to understand human purpose and meaning. Augustinian spirituality is both deeply rooted in the mystery of Christ and radically open to human restlessness and spiritual striving. "Augustinian spirituality, developed over time, and enriched by the example and teachings of our forebears, ought to be lived according to the circumstances of time, place, and culture and in harmony with our charism" (*Constitutions of the Order of Saint Augustine* I.2.16). We can expect Augustinian spirituality and its reception to continue to evolve, as the Church and the world advance toward situations and questions that await us in the future.

While this book draws on the academic work of many scholars, it approaches Augustine's thought from the perspective of spirituality. That means it examines human meaning and values; it asks about our ultimate purpose or end; and it explores relationship with God, the source of our being. Spirituality is a highly subjective topic to which we all—you, me, and Augustine—bring our own experience, perspective, and predilections. In his book *The Trinity*, Augustine calls the relationship between author and reader a "covenant both prudent and pious" (*Trin* I.1.5). To honor such a "covenant," I suggest slow, meditative reading that allows you the time to reflect on the many quotations from Augustine, and the space to evaluate his ideas in light of your own insight and judgment. The goal is not to convince you, but to engage you.

Accordingly, this book nurtures a twofold hope. The first is to evoke responses from the worldwide Augustinian family, with its great diversity of cultures, languages, and experiences across six continents. There is not one homogenous understanding or uniform experience of Augustinian spirituality, at any given time or place in its history. This volume, shaped in a contemporary American Catholic context, will benefit from ongoing dialogue among Augustinians everywhere.

The second hope is for wider dialogue. The nature of Augustine's understanding of the restless human heart invites insight from those whose spiritualities are lived beyond the boundaries of the Catholic Church or any Christian Church. Such dialogue will enrich the spiritual legacy of the Bishop of Hippo. All those whose hearts are restless in the pursuit of truth are worthy dialogue partners in conversations about Augustinian spirituality. They all witness to God's loving providence that carries us along our pilgrim way (*Conf* IV.16.31), caring "for each of us as though each were the only one, and for all alike with the same tenderness you show to each" (*Conf* III.11.20).

Pope Leo XIV has become the most famous Augustinian in the world today. He brings to the Petrine ministry an Augustinian life of contemplation in community, spirituality amidst service, and humility with hospitality for all who seek God. Augustinian spirituality shaped him as a friar and formed him as a pastor. He now brings this spirituality to the notice of the Universal Church and indeed to all who look to him as a moral and spiritual leader. His pontificate opens a new chapter in the Augustinian tradition and provides a global context for Augustinian spirituality. He has invited all of us, Augustinians, Catholics, Christians, members of all religions, and all people of goodwill to walk forward together with hope, following the pilgrim path that is our earthly journey into the fullness of God, "the Sabbath of eternal life" (*Conf* XIII.36.51).

# Part One

## Communion

Augustinian spirituality attends to prayer, restlessness, and questions of the human heart. At the same time, it reaches beyond the experience of the self to the mystery of the soul. Chapters one to three present Augustine's discovery of interiority and his turn from worldly ambition to the true source of human happiness and fulfillment in God. They explore Augustine's encounter with Christ and his conversion and graced participation in the sacrificial love of God.

Augustinian spirituality is also an encounter with others, since all humanity is united in, through, and with Christ. "We who are many are *one in him, who is one*" (*Ex Ps* 127.3). Faith leads us to loving contemplation on the mystery of God, to ongoing conversion of life in response to divine love, and to loving communion with each other.

O to love! To go and be lost to self! To reach God!
*Sermon* 159.8

*O amare! O ire! O sibi perire! O ad Deum pervenire!*

# Chapter One

# The Mystery of Christ

At the very beginning of Saint Augustine's *Confessions*, he presents three intertwining themes, three spiritual inclinations. They are prayer, restlessness, and questioning. They persist throughout the rest of *Confessions.* Like three melodic counterpoints in a piece of music, they emerge and recede, retiring then returning, giving way to each other, drawing us into the compelling complexities of Augustine's mind and heart. They are persistent dynamics in Augustinian spirituality.

As Augustine relates various episodes from his life, he constantly reprises these three themes. The narrative portions of *Confessions* are suffused with prayer. Augustine tells us how he prayed earnestly during critical turning points in his life. He admits the restlessness that agitated his heart amidst times of change and challenge. He discloses the many questions prompted by events in his life and questions what was really happening within him as things changed around him. *Confessions* is not an autobiography in our modern sense of the genre, which is a historical account of someone's life. It is more. It is an invitation for readers to join Augustine by reflecting on their own lives in light of these three predispositions of the soul: prayer, restlessness, and questioning.

Augustine is confident that God attends to our prayers, understands our restlessness, and receives our questions. He asks that God aid everyone in this spiritual quest, so that each person might "hear the truth about oneself from You" (*Conf* X.3.3). He cherishes this hope for all his readers, for all those who are "the companions of my joy and sharers in my mortality, my fellow citizens still on pilgrimage with me, those who have gone before and those who will follow, and all who bear me company in my life" (*Conf* X.4.6). To reflect more deeply on these three dynamics of Augustinian spirituality, let us consider each in turn.

## Prayer

Augustine begins *Confessions* with prayer: "Great are you, O Lord, and exceedingly worthy of praise; your power is immense, and your wisdom beyond reckoning" (Psalms 48:1; 96:4; 145:3). He affirms that prayer is part of being human, an instinct in our nature. "We humans, who are a due part of your creation, long to praise you" (*Conf* I.1.1). Prayer is not an add-on to our humanity. Its source is our souls, not our religion. Religion might provide valuable keys to unlock prayer, specific language to voice it, and primordial symbols to express it. But prayer and spirituality are, in Augustine's understanding, already part of who we are, how we are made, and what we have been created for. To pray is one of the most natural things for human beings to do.

Augustine's favorite prayers were the Hebrew psalms. He begins *Confessions* with passages from multiple psalms. The psalms weave their way in and out of each of the thirteen books of his *Confessions*. They provide Augustine with inspired words and phrases to capture every human emotion, and then to lift them all to God in prayer. In fact, the longest collection of his writings on any subject is his *Expositions of the Psalms*. These are homilies and meditations that ponder, mull over, and explore the psalms as prayers rising to God from the depths of the human heart.

For Augustine, prayer and the human emotions and feelings that move us to pray are natural parts of a spiritual life. The power of the divine within us emerges, erupts, and surges through human affect. True, our emotions and feelings can go awry and wreak havoc on ourselves and others. Hence the need to bring them into the prayer they have prompted, where grace can tame, tutor, and transform their power to work for our good and that of others. He prays that our affect might become an agent of love, and that we, "during the pilgrimage of this life, . . . will have all these emotions in the right way" (*CG* XIV.9). For Augustine, our affective lives are not only an essential dimension of our spiritual lives. They are invitations to prayer through which God sanctifies our feelings, desires, and longings.

## Restlessness

Augustine's heartfelt opening prayer in *Confessions* immediately leads to his second theme of restlessness. "You arouse us so that praising you may bring us joy, because you have made us and drawn us to yourself, and our heart is unquiet until it rests in You" (*Conf* I.1.1). Our feelings, our emotions, our affect—all human sentiments—stir or disturb our hearts, leaving them *inquietum*. *Inquietum* is his Latin word that describes our nature as ever restless, often distracted, sometimes unsettled, or ominously out of sorts.

Augustine locates this restlessness not only within our hearts. It is not only the product of our inner thoughts and furtive feelings. Restlessness is also outside, in the world. And echoes from what is outside us often resound within us. We live enmeshed in overlapping environments, immersed in psycho-social matrices. There is so much *inquietum* circling, swirling around us. So many demands made of us, so many expectations coming at us, so many responsibilities put on us by others, our jobs, the world in general. No doubt if Augustine were alive today, he would note how the din of human restlessness has grown exponentially into a cyber uproar spinning round the globe, creating social superstorms, stirring tornadoes of emotion, opinion, and domination—hurricanes of *inquietum* that assail our hearts and "engulf us in whirlpools of sins" (*Conf* II.2.2).

This external restlessness can do two things to our already restless hearts. It can provoke them even more: From outside, it can invade our hearts, distract our minds, rattle our brains, and so increase our *internal* restlessness. It can leave our hearts skipping beats, out of rhythm with who we are or want to be. The demands of the world can make us "miserable, apprehensive, full of foreboding and torn with cares," as Augustine described himself when he was the imperial rhetorician in Milan (*Conf* VI.6.9–10).

Or what might be worse, all the external noise can anesthetize our hearts. It can distract us from our inner life, make us immune to our inner restlessness, and alienate us from our own affections. The world can administer a spiritual sedative, put us in a cyber coma, render us unresponsive to our own hearts. It can leave us unaware of our own feelings and thoughts, detached from our own choices, deadened by an unnatural sleep induced by the din around us. We lie prostrate, impassive, and indifferent. Augustine prescribes the therapy of the Divine Physician who can jumpstart our restless hearts to wake us from our spiritual stupor and revive our spirit (*Conf* VII.8.12). We need the One who can call, shout, break through our deafness, banish our blindness, and restore our breath so that, gasping for life, we can once again taste and touch the divine (*Conf* X.27.38). We need to be restored to our natural, internal, spiritual restlessness.

## Questioning

Augustinian *inquietum* reaches from the heart into the mind. A restless heart resonates in restive reason. It stimulates an inquisitive intellect. It provokes questions. Scores of these heartfelt questions emerge in book one of *Confessions*. They fill the paragraphs immediately after Augustine's opening prayer and the disclosure of his restless heart. He poses questions about God and prayer: "Grant me to know and understand, Lord, which comes first: to call upon you or to praise you? To know you or to call upon you? Must we know you before we can call upon you?" (*Conf* I.1.1). "What are you, then, my God?" (I.4.4). "Where are you?" (I.2.2; 3.3). He questions faith: "How can people call upon someone in whom they do not yet believe?" (I.1.1). He wonders about himself and what he means to God: "What indeed am I to you?" (I.5.5). There are questions about religion: "What does anyone who speaks of you really say?" (I.4.4). Questions about the earth and creation: "I questioned everything it held" (X.6.9). And so on and on, throughout all thirteen books of his *Confessions*; seemingly endless questioning.

In commenting on Augustine's theology, scholars have remarked that Augustine thinks in questions. We can also say that he prays in questions. "My questioning was my attentive spirit" (*Conf* X.6.9). *Confessions* has been described as one long prayer of Augustine to God, one long prayerful conversation with God. All throughout his prayer, he invites us to eavesdrop on his questions. As we listen to him pray, we witness his inquiries of God, his restless questions to his Lord. True, questions may imply doubt and uncertainty; and difficult questions may mark a stalemate or standoff between the questioner and God. But questions, even questions about God or to God, are not inimical to a spiritual life. They are evidence of engagement with it, expression of our potential as spiritual beings. For Augustine, questions of God are part of our human nature, an inevitable dynamic in our restless hearts and restive minds. They are appropriate to a spiritual life.

Theologian Paul Tillich wrote that doubt and faith are two sides of the same coin. Augustinian spirituality might suggest a different analogy: Our questions, even our doubts, are goads to faith, spurs that keep us moving forward. They are part of the kit we carry with us in our pilgrim backpacks. Questions lead to conversation, conversation to engagement, engagement to community, and community to pilgrimage, that is, to moving forward together in the quest for truth. We question because we wonder, and that wonder moves us ever closer to one another and to the future that God prepares for us and pledges to us through the gift of the Holy Spirit (*CG* XIX.17).

Augustinian spirituality is an ongoing exploration of the mystery of our human nature, a restless desire to discover who we are and the reason for our existence. No matter where we are in our own spiritual pilgrimage, no matter how far along we may have already traveled, in one sense, we are always still at the beginning. We are all still on the first page of the first book of *Confessions*, praying, restless, and questioning. Augustinian spirituality embraces an *inquietum* that will be satisfied only in being loved infinitely and loving eternally. It is a restless questioning that will only find rest in the "supreme sabbath which has no evening, . . . where we shall be still and see, see and love, love and praise . . . in the end without end" (*CG* XXII.30).

## Grace

In the meantime, we pray. We are restless. We question. We make our way through life, striving to stay on the path of love, seeking God's face (Psalm 105:4; *Trin* I.1.5). However, as we travel on our spiritual path, we make unexpected discoveries. We encounter what we can call moments of grace. Something unanticipated happens, something not planned or even likely. Something not of our own making or imagination. A startling image breaks into our prayer. A quiet peace calms our restless heart. An insight emerges amidst a question. A friend's casual remark gets us pondering. We may not know how, why, or whence such events come to us. We do know they can spark significant change. They can guide us to a spiritual crossroad and indicate a new direction. In *Confessions*, Augustine tells us about such graced moments in his own journey of faith, and how he eventually discerned in them the presence of God.

Augustine always believed in God. "I always believed in your existence and your care for us, even though I did not know what to think about your essential nature . . ." (*Conf* VI.5.8). His conversion was not from atheism to theism. Like many spiritual seekers in his own day as well as in ours, he accepted the existence of God, even of a providential, caring God. But, again like many people then and now, he had questions about the nature of God, and about how to relate to such a Being.

As we all do in our childhood, the boy Augustine cherished naïve images of God. He prayed that God would save him from beatings at school and help him win scholastic contests. His was a childlike and childish spirituality. Then, as a young man, he rejected the devotional African Christianity of his mother, Monica, and displayed an urbane disdain for simple believers of all stripes. He ridiculed what he labeled the literary inferiority of the Bible. Accordingly, he adopted the intriguing mythology of the Manicheans, and their thinly spiritualistic, anti-materialistic God. He soon grew tired of their tantalizing theories but idly tolerated them for many years "in default of anything better" (*Conf* V.10.18).

Eventually, Augustine admitted his disaffection with Manichean teaching. In a somewhat stubborn reaction against their doctrinaire preaching, he adopted philosophical skepticism. He mistrusted teachers from any school of thought and doubted the possibility of ever reaching any true understanding of God. It is as if he stopped asking questions. At least he gave up hope of any satisfactory answers. He hushed his restlessness under the spell of suspicion. We might even say that, for a while, he abandoned the spiritual life. Then something unanticipated happened. A moment of grace.

During his years as the court rhetorician in Milan, Augustine came to know the lettered Christians of that city who read a philosophy that was quite different from the skepticism he had adopted. These Christians studied ideas found in the blend of Greek philosophy that today we call Neoplatonism. They recognized Augustine's intelligence and the earnestness of this successful young courtier who had come from the outback of North Africa to take an important job at the very center of the Empire. They also knew he was reconsidering Christianity. Encouraged by Bishop Ambrose and his priest Simplicianus, these philosophically inclined Christians introduced Augustine to "some books by the Platonists" (*Conf* VII.9.13).

Augustine started reading. He found these ancient Greek philosophers to be like him: restless souls who questioned God even as they prayed. He studied their ideas about God, and about how one might strive toward an encounter with, or at least some understanding of this mysterious Being who was the source of all being. He learned about the varieties of mystical disciplines—today we might call them spiritualities—found among the writings of these philosophers. His introduction to Neoplatonism was a turning point, a crossroad, a moment of grace. His encounter with their philosophical and spiritual teachings restarted the skeptical

Augustine's spiritual life and set him off in a new direction, questioning, restless, and praying.

Augustine tells us that he tried one of the meditative exercises espoused in the mystical teachings of Neoplatonism. His attempt at contemplation led him to a powerful spiritual experience:

> I entered, then, and with the vision of my spirit, such as it was, I saw the incommutable light far above my spiritual ken, transcending my mind: not this common light . . . but something different, utterly different. . . . this very light made me, and I was below it because by it I was made. Anyone who knows truth knows it, and whoever knows it knows eternity. Love knows it. (*Conf* VII.10.16)

A second attempt at this meditative exercise brought him to another encounter with divine light. "And then my mind attained to *That Which Is*, in the flash of one tremulous glance" (*Conf* VII.17.23). These were mystical experiences, a spiritual interiority he had never before imagined. However, they were fleeting encounters. Augustine admits that he did not have the strength to sustain these sporadic contemplative moments. "I was forced back through weakness and returned to my familiar surroundings, bearing with me a loving memory, one that yearned for something of which I had caught the fragrance, but could not yet feast upon" (*Conf* VII.17.23).

Despite his inability to prolong and maintain a contemplative state, these experiences changed him. They guided his search for truth to a crossroad and goaded him to take a new direction. In these graced moments, Augustine pierced through the shadows of this life to the brightness of the beginning, to the Light at the beginning, to the first source of being, to *That Which Is*. Questions about God once again stirred his mind to new inquiry. In book seven of *Confessions*, he tells us how his discovery of Neoplatonic mysticism encouraged such questions once again (*Conf* VII.10.16). His confrontation with "real, unchangeable truth, which is eternal" rejuvenated his discursive reason (*Conf* VII.10.16; 17.23). His mystical experience of prayerful encounter with the mystery of God, with "incommutable light far above my spiritual ken," moved him to pray in new ways. All this resuscitated his restless heart.

Looking back on this period in his life, Augustine acknowledged the presence and power of divine grace in these events. He believed God used these "books of the Platonists" to prepare him to read "your scriptures" (*Conf* VII.20.26). It was at that point that another moment of grace entered his life. This event erupted with explosive force and left him standing astounded and exposed on his spiritual landscape. He turned his attention from the books of the Platonists to the Gospel of John.

## Christ

Amidst the spiritual ferment stirred by Neoplatonism, Augustine heard about people whose response to the Christian faith involved a radical dedication of their lives to Christ and the Gospel. A fellow courtier named Ponticianus visited Augustine one day. He told him the story about Antony of Egypt and the many Christians who, like Antony, responded without hesitation to Christ's command to "Go and sell all you possess and give the money to the poor: [Y]ou will have treasure in heaven. Then come, follow me" (Matthew 19:21). Neoplatonism had revived Augustine's spiritual life. Now the story of Antony turned his attention to Christ, and to questions about Christ. Who exactly was Jesus Christ? What about him could inspire people to such a radical response?

This was not the first time Augustine had questions about Christ. He confesses how in the years before their Baptism, both he and his friend Alypius struggled to understand Christian teaching about the nature of Christ (*Conf* VII.18.24–20.26). They disagreed and argued whether Christ was human or divine, or some mixture of both. Augustine confesses that, in those earlier years, his various understandings of Christ were quite unorthodox.

Then he tells us how his journey of faith reached a new turning point, another moment of grace. His spiritual path took a radical turn when he read the Gospel of John, one that was to be decisive and permanent. He found in John something he had not found in books of philosophy. It astonished him. The importance Augustine attributes to this discovery is evident in his extensive citation of John's Gospel in book seven of *Confessions*. He quotes John at length:

> In the beginning was the Word, and the Word was with God; he was God. He was with God in the beginning. Everything was made through him; nothing came to be without him. What was made was alive with his life, and that life was the light of humankind. The Light shines in the darkness, and the darkness has never been able to master it. (John 1:1-5; *Conf* VII.9.13)

Augustine continues and highlights the climax of John's prologue: "The Word was made flesh and dwelt among us" (John 1:14). The "incommutable light far above my spiritual ken" was no longer remote, requiring Herculean human effort to reach through disciplined contemplation. That Word, that Light, that divinity "dwelt among us" in the person of Jesus of Nazareth. God spoke "real, unchangeable truth, which is eternal" in Christ, the Word Made Flesh (*Conf* VII.10.16; 17.23).

For Augustine, this changed everything. Nothing could ever be the same, not his prayer, not his restlessness, not his questions. It is not that these spiritual dynamics resolved or dissolved. They were transformed. It is a radically new beginning for Augustine, for his life and his spirituality. The inaccessible Light of God, the Word through whom all things were made, overcame the infinite distance between divine and human, and "was made flesh."

For the rest of his life and his ministry, Augustine dwells on the mystery of the Incarnation, the ever-astounding Truth that the transcendent, incomprehensible, and infinite One humbly became one with us in creation and history. Augustine needed no longer to rely solely on mystical exercises of the soul, straining to reach the incommutable light far above his spiritual talent, striving to transcend his mind, to leave the flesh of his body behind. The Word took on flesh. The Light had come to him and pierced his darkness.

The teaching of Christ as the Word Made Flesh, fully human and fully divine, was an invitation to enter the spiritual mystery which the doctrine expressed. Years later, in his sermons, Augustine encouraged his congregation to this same encounter with the Word Made Flesh. As he preaches on the feast of Christmas, he moves from the ecclesial prose of the creed, "begotten not made, consubstantial with the Father," to the spiritual poetry of faith. In Jesus, we encounter "God at our feet," the mystery of "divinity grown weak" (*Conf* VII.18.24). His Christmas homilies burst with verses of wonderment at this mystery. "The Wisdom of God presented itself to us as an infant, and the Word of God uttered the flesh as its voice. . . . For whose benefit did such sublimity come in such humility? . . . totally for ours. Wake up, humankind, for you God became man. . . . For you, I repeat, God became man" (*S* 185.1). In another Christmas sermon, he urges:

> What praises, then, should we be singing to God's love, what thanks should we be expressing! I mean, he loved us so much that for our sake he came to be in time, though all times were made through him; and he was prepared to be younger in age than many of his servants in the world. He loved us so much that he became man though he had made man; that he was created from a mother whom he had created, carried in arms he had fashioned, sucked breasts which he himself filled; that he lay squalling in a manger wordless in infancy, though he is the Word without whom human eloquence would be at a loss for words. (S 188.2)

Christ is the mystery at the center of Augustinian spirituality. All of Augustine's spiritual life and theology can be understood and interpreted in light of his discovery of the message of the Gospel:

God's unbounded love for us revealed in "the man Jesus Christ, the mediator between God and humankind" (*Conf* VII.18.24). The Incarnation is the eruption of divine love, emerging into time, breaking the boundaries of the universe, permeating our being, our awareness, our past, present, and future. Augustine writes in book ten of *Confessions*, "You pierced my heart with your word, and I fell in love with you" (*Conf* X.6.8). The word that pierces his restless heart is the Word Made Flesh.

In reflecting back on these moments of discovery and revelation in his spiritual journey, Augustine discerns the loving presence of God, powerful and persistent, yet at the same time gentle and patient. These changes were not of his making, not of his merit, or from his imagination. They were of God, God working through the kind regard of others, the loving care of community, and the inspired text of Scripture. "Look for merit there, look for a cause, look for justice; and see whether you can find anything but grace" (*S* 185.4).

## Sanctified

Belief in the Incarnation transposes the humanism of Augustinian spirituality into a new key of faith. The historical event of the Word made flesh sanctifies the three dynamics of the spiritual life. In light of the Incarnation, prayer, restlessness, and questioning evolve and emerge in new ways, enlightened and empowered by the mysteries of grace.

Prayer is no longer simply the cry of an ardent soul lifting mind and heart to a distant God. Prayer becomes a divine prerogative. By sharing in our humanity, Christ adopts our prayers as his own. The inspired language of the psalms we use to express our prayer in all its pressing affect is also Christ's prayer with us and for us to the Father. The words and sentiments of our prayer become words and sentiments of the "mediator between God and humankind" (*Conf* VII.18.24). We pray now through, with, and in Christ. Our prayers enter immediately into the divine heart, "even before a word is on my tongue" (Psalm 139:4).

Restlessness is no longer the lonely, existential crisis of a human heart yearning for a distant, unreachable God. Christ is the revelation that God shares our restlessness. Christ is eternally restless for us, endlessly reaching out to us, passionately yearning for union with us, a "Love ever burning, never extinguished" (*Conf* X.29.40). God, in divine fashion, is restless, "never new, never old, renewing all things . . . ever active, ever at rest . . . " The sacred heart is *inquietum* for us, "loving without frenzy, jealous yet secure, regretful without sadness, angry yet tranquil . . ." (*Conf* I.4.4).

Questioning is no longer simply outward-looking inquiry. The Incarnation of God in Christ transforms our questions by infusing them with the "Light that came into the world." Our questions are enlightened by faith, by "that faith which you have kindled lamp-like, on my nocturnal path" (*Conf* XIII.14.15). Faith illumines the depths of our soul (*Sol* I.1.2: 8.15). Our questions come alive with divine life, the same infinite life that is the light of humankind. Divine life and light illuminate the dimness of our inquiry, so that darkness, skepticism, and despair will never be able to overcome us (John 1:1-5). Christian hope bolsters, intensifies, and advances all our questions.

In these ways, Augustinian spirituality is an invitation to a deeper humanism, transfigured and transformed by the power of the Holy Spirit. We might call it a humanism sanctified by grace. It is an invitation to discover the transcendent Eternal One in the immanent depths of the human. It is a revelation of the Holy Spirit of God stirring at the source of our being, abiding at the genesis of our nature, hovering over the depths of our soul. What else could the Incarnation mean? The Word become flesh is the revelation that flesh can receive the Word. The Incarnation affirms a radical interpretation of the claim in Genesis that "God created humankind in his image, in the image of God he created them; male and female he created them" (Genesis 1:27). The Incarnation reveals a whole new dimension to the nature and potential of who we are as God's image sanctified by the Spirit (*Conf* XIII.22.32–33).

# Pride

The creation stories recounted in Genesis 1 and 2 present an uplifting vision of humanity. We are made in the image of God, inspired by the breath of God (2:7). However, things fall apart in Genesis 3. It tells the story of what Augustine famously called "original sin," the sin at the origin of humankind. Given Augustine's extensive theological reflections on original sin and its effects, it should be no surprise that Augustinian spirituality takes account of sin and how it can compromise the spiritual life.

Augustine studies the story of the fall in Genesis 3 to discover "the spiritual meaning" behind its "veil of mystery" (*Conf* VI.4.6). His interpretation of Genesis 3 is symbolic or analogical. He probes the ancient Hebrew narrative for its wisdom, wisdom inspired by God working through the biblical authors for our enlightenment. Augustine searches the text with an ardent longing to discover "the inner meaning of your words." He prays for God's blessing on his restless quest for understanding the text (*Conf* XI.2.4).

Augustine looks beyond the behavior of Adam and Eve and searches for their motive. He quickly identifies it as pride. Pride is the original sin of Adam and Eve. They disobey God's command "not to eat of the fruit of the tree in the middle of the garden" because they want "to be like God, knowing good and evil" (Genesis 3:5). As Augustine reads it, the meaning of Genesis 3 is that humanity usurped its own origin, assumed its own priority, and seized control of its future. God's original vision for our kind quickly came to an end. Pride, therefore, is the "mother of all sins" (*Hom Gos Jn* 25.16).

Augustine identifies the results of this primordial presumption. He names the lasting effects of this original sin: ignorance and weakness. "Error and weakness. Either you don't know what to do, and you go wrong, you fall into error; or else you know what should be done, and you are overpowered by weakness" (*S* 182.6). These effects, he claims, are inter-generational. They have infected every human heart throughout all of history (*Misc Smp* 1.11). So, "intermixed and intermingled" (*CG* I.35) with our natural spiritual instincts of prayer, restlessness, and questioning lie the threats of ignorance and weakness. They are endemic in human habit and destructive of human spirituality. And so, we humans are beset by "inveterate custom," with two wills fighting it out—"the old and the new, the one carnal, the other spiritual"—and in the struggle our souls get torn apart (*Conf* VIII.5.10).

Although Augustinian spirituality identifies our innate predispositions toward prayer, restlessness, and questioning as universal potentials, it also accounts for their corruption. Prayer can become a transactional exercise of power plays with God, holy bargaining for a good deal because we believe fortune owes us. Restlessness can wander far afield, seeking satisfaction through inordinate indulgence in power, domination, or lust. Questioning can devolve into idle curiosity, gossip, and deceit, abandoning the search for truth. Spirituality must take account of the dark side of our nature, the prideful love of self to the detriment of neighbor and even contempt of God (*CG* XIV.28). It is no wonder that in the *Monastic Rule*, Augustine warns that "pride lurks even in good works, in order to destroy them" (*Rule* I.8).

Augustinian spirituality advises a prudence born of experience. It laments that the divine image in which we have been made by God, and remade in Christ, is more often than not obscured and distorted—though not erased—by human pride and its miscreant twin offsprings, ignorance and weakness. It warns that our spiritual nature can be compromised, our spiritual journey set off track, misdirected, and brought to a dead end. Augustine's own experience was that the flesh—his flesh—needed redemption, help, grace from the Word Made Flesh. The only treatment for original pride, he says, is the Incarnation, the humility of God in Christ, "God at our feet." The Incarnation is not just revelation. It is remedy. It is the cure for our spiritual infirmity, for our ignorance, and our weakness. Divine love, perfected by taking on the weakness of our flesh, heals and strengthens us so that we can ascend the way opened by the Incarnation, and resume our journey along the pilgrim road to God.

Christ is the essence of Light, inaccessible and incommutable, now made flesh, now accessible amidst the contingencies of our existence. Jesus is the expression of divine love brought to perfection in the weakness of humility (*Trin* IV.1.2). The Word Made Flesh is the "certain pure outflow of the glory of the Almighty" (Wisdom 7:25-26; *Trin* IV.5.27). The One from whom all things come is infinite love, endless self-donation, eternal outpouring of being. *That Which Is* is love.

In its fullness, Augustinian spirituality is a response to God's love for us expressed in and through Christ. That divine love overcomes our pride, enlightens our minds, empowers our wills, and makes us capable of knowing and loving God in return. But what is the nature of our response? What is the nature of conversion to Christ?

## Chapter Two

# Conversion

In chapter one, we saw how Augustine identified prayer, restlessness, and questioning as innate predispositions of our nature, signals of spirituality at the source of our being. We also recalled Augustine's graced encounter with the Word Made Flesh in Jesus Christ, and the critical role of Christ in Augustinian spirituality. Encounter with Christ transforms our spiritual nature. It unites our prayer with his. It redeems our restlessness by revealing God's passion for us. It suffuses our questions with the divine light that illuminates our souls.

In this second chapter, we examine Augustine's response to Christ. Building on his experience as recounted in *Confessions*, we look at three actions that comprise that response. The first is decision: a graced exercise of our will. Augustine's analysis of the will and its interaction with divine grace is a window into his spirituality. The second act, in response to the Word Made Flesh, is conversion. We will reflect on conversion as a particular kind of decision, a spiritual decision of surrender and sacrifice. After decision and conversion, the third act in our response to the Gospel is Baptism. It is the sacrament that expresses and effects our incorporation into Christ. It makes us one with him and with all who believe in him and indeed with all humankind.

## Decision

Decision is a faculty that pervades human experience. It emerges early in life. Toddlers soon discover their capacity for will, and roundly exercise it. They learn to signal—to demand—what they want, often against parental wishes and wisdom. Later, adolescents cautiously explore choices and anxiously test their capacity to make decisions, despite peer pressure and social coercion. Young adults face crucial decisions about their partners, friends, and jobs; about where and how to live. Older adults reflect back on the consequences their choices have had both for themselves and for others. Toward the end of life, decisions still loom. Healthcare, legacies, and final rites want attention and demand decisions. We can debate all we want about free will and determinism. But we can't avoid making decisions, unless we default to passivity or indifference, which are in themselves choices with their own consequences.

*Confessions* is full of stories about decisions that Augustine made over his first thirty years. As for most of us, the early decisions affecting his life were made by his parents. When he was eight, he had a serious fever and begged to be baptized. Following the custom of the time, his parents decided against Baptism, counting on his recovery and preferring to wait until after the stormy years of adolescence (*Conf* I.11.17–18). Looking back, he asks about their motivation in withholding Baptism and judges it misguided.

They also made decisions about his schooling. When Augustine was eleven, they sent him away to the city of Madauros for more education (*Conf* II.3.5). After they ran out of tuition money, he had to return home for a year. He was sixteen. It turned out to be a year of bad decisions. His sexuality "surged" like the "flood-tide" of a "stormy sea," as he "frothed and floundered" in fornication, and engaged in "various furtive love affairs" and "disreputable amours" (*Conf* II.1.1–3.8). He scrutinizes both his own lust and his parents' tolerance.

Suddenly, in book two, he turns his attention from adolescent ache to petty theft. He tells the story of how one night he and his mates stole pears from the orchard of a neighbor. Augustine spends pages analyzing his motivation for such a choice. "What did I love in you, O my theft, what did I love in you, the nocturnal crime of my sixteenth year?" (*Conf* II.6.12). The pears were not particularly ripe and tasty. Did he do it simply because it was off limits? "Could

I have found pleasure in that?" (*Conf* II.6.14). Was it peer pressure? "As I recall my state of mind at the time, I would not have done it alone; I most certainly would not have done it alone" (*Conf* II.8.16).

Amidst this persistent questioning, the hint of an answer about his motivation peeks through. He describes the theft as "a shady parody of omnipotence by getting away with something forbidden" (*Conf* II.6.14). In the very next sentence, he mentions Adam's decision to eat the forbidden fruit. Augustine in the pear orchard of a neighbor is an allusion to Adam in the garden of Eden (Genesis 3:3). Augustine's theft is a "shady parody" of Adam and Eve's original sin of pride when they strove to be "like God, knowing good and evil," in other words omnipotent (Genesis 3:5). Their sin was a bold exercise of pride in primordial daylight. Augustine's theft was a murky mix of pride and other impulses under the cover of darkness.

As mentioned in chapter one, Augustine perceived two lasting results in all human beings due to the original sin of pride: ignorance of mind and weakness of will. In the story of the theft of pears, he identifies both these effects of original sin in his own behavior.

***Ignorance.*** While Augustine's account of the theft of pears may have been a true story, he constructs the narrative about his adolescent ignorance in order to reflect at length on human ignorance in general. Like those rascals roaming around Thagaste at night, all of us can be habitually oblivious, carelessly mindless, trampling our neighbor's rights and absconding with what is theirs. As Augustine examines his conscience, he closely inspects the ignorance that weaves in and out of his mixed, uncertain motives, creeping like a destructive vine rooted in the soil of pride. Pride, the presumption of our own priority and the relentless quest for control, strangles our intuition of the good and chokes our insight into what is just.

Our intelligence, says Augustine, was created blameless and without defect. But it is "darkened" by pride, so that we lose all sense of proportion and order (*Nat Gr* 3.3). Goodness and justice are eclipsed by the shadow of pride. They disappear in the obscurity of ignorance. Inveterate habit keeps our eyes dim and accustomed to the gloom (*Misc Smp* 1.10). "Who can teach me, except the One who illumines my heart and distinguishes between its shadows?" (*Conf* II.8.16).

***Weakness of Will.*** The other result of original pride is weakness of will. Even when we might know the good and right thing to do, we do not have the strength of will to follow through (*Forg Sins Bap Lit* II.17.26). This was the main point of the later disagreement between Augustine and the British monk Pelagius. Pelagius taught that divine grace enlightens our minds and so overcomes the darkness of our ignorance. God teaches us the good and right thing to do. Then, Pelagius claims, it is up to us to do it. He advises a spiritual life of asceticism, of fervent prayer, much abstinence, and regular fasting so that we can strengthen our wills to do what God teaches us. It is an athletic spirituality of practice and performance.

Augustine agrees with Pelagius that we need God's grace for enlightenment. But he disagrees with Pelagius's "just do it" spirituality of self-insured will power. Augustine applauds Pelagius's acknowledgment of grace in attaining knowledge of the good and the just, but laments his failure to understand that our will, like our mind, is also weakened by original pride and needs God's help. "He attributes the smaller of these two gifts [knowledge] to divine help, while he wrongly claims the greater [will] for human choice" (*Gr Chr Org Sin* I.26.27).

One of the key points in Augustine's spirituality is that God strengthens our will to help us choose the good and the just. He often cites a passage from the Book of Proverbs: "The will is prepared by the Lord (Proverbs 8:35)" (*Ans Jul* III.114). But how? How does divine grace strengthen our wills so that we can make decisions that serve goodness and advance justice? How does God empower our wills?

It is a matter of love. Augustine believed that we choose to do the right and good thing ultimately because we love it. We find delight in doing it. "Each person obeys the commandments of God . . . only with love. . . . Only God gives this love, for love comes from God (1 John 4:7)" (*Ans Jul* III.114). In Christ, we discover and experience God's infinite, unconditional love for us. This discovery changes everything. Our experience of God's eternal love for us in

Christ breaks down the defenses of our pride and breaks through to the center of our being, "like a sword penetrating us to the core" (*Conf* IX.2.3). This love not only enlightens our minds to know what is good and just. God's love for us strengthens our wills to do the good and the just.

Divine love does not supersede our wills. Rather, it gently, quietly, almost imperceptibly awakens within us an attraction toward the good and the just. They become desirable. We not only know them. We love them. God's love, as it were, loves the good and the just through us. We come to see as God sees. We come to love as God loves. And we desire to act accordingly. Our free will remains intact and capable of freely choosing what the light of grace renders appealing and desirable. Augustine's theology of the will opens onto his spirituality of grace. For Augustine, the spiritual life involves an ever-growing realization that God loves us unreservedly, unconditionally, infinitely (*Ans Jul* VI.10.11). That love "prepares our will" by drawing our attention to what is good and just, coaxing us, "tempting" us with an emergent love for the innate power of goodness and justice.

Augustinian spirituality finds the encounter with divine love so radical and pervasive that it disarms our pride, clears our mind, and inclines our will toward God and the well-being of all God's creation. In that sense, Augustinian spirituality is effortless. It is not a spiritual life of striving to achieve holiness through good works, or of hoping to impress God by sacrifice. It is not a spirituality of dogged decisions, of laboring to merit acceptance and redemption by our own efforts. It is a joyful response born of the infinite love that affirms our innate value, restores our discernment, and inclines our will toward goodness and justice, rousing our restless hearts to move in that direction, gently aligning our decisions with the divine.

## Conversion

After the story about stealing pears, Augustine shares many other stories about his decisions. He tells of his life as a student and then a teacher in the city of Carthage. He recalls his long-term relationship with his companion of thirteen years and remembers the son whom they shared and loved. He talks about his decision to travel from Africa to Rome in search of advancement, deceiving his widowed mother and leaving her devastated by his departure. He reports his ultimate success at the height of his profession as the rhetorician of the imperial court at Milan. He laments the separation from the woman he loved, his engagement to a trophy wife, and a temporary liaison with another woman. Questions about his motivation persist throughout these accounts. He admits a stubborn inability to live honestly, responsibly, and authentically, and confesses unbridled ambition and egotism. He recollects his uncertainty about what he really wanted or should want. He regrets the restless indecision and persistent apprehension that plagued him despite his professional success (*Conf* VI.6.9). He admits, "I had become a great enigma to myself" (*Conf* IV.4.9).

The most famous story he tells is about his most famous decision: to follow Christ. He relates this dramatic turn in his spiritual life at the end of book eight of *Confessions*.The conversion scene is the garden of his home in Milan. For months, he had been struggling with multiple questions about Christian faith. His restlessness had crescendoed to agony over his hesitation, and to anxiety over his addiction to power and pleasure. His prayers had assumed an air of desperation. He was "at odds with myself, and fragmenting myself. . . . This disintegration was occurring without my consent" (*Conf* VIII.10.22). Despite his contemplative experiences with Neoplatonism and his growing acceptance of the revelation of God's love in Christ as proclaimed in the Gospel of John, he still held back from giving his life over to Christ in full self-donation. Augustine resisted what he sensed lay above and beyond any profession of faith. He held back from a spiritual and moral conversion. He feared living deeply in the mystery of Christ.

He carried all this turmoil into the garden of his house in Milan on a spring day in 386. After sharing his dismay with his friend Alypius, he withdrew and flung himself down under a fig tree—an allusion to Scripture—his eyes overflowing with tears, his mind bursting with questions, "O Lord, how long? How long? . . . Why must I go on saying, 'Tomorrow . . . tomorrow'? Why not now?" (*Conf* VIII.12.28).

Then something unexpected happens. Something unimagined by Augustine's restless heart, unpredicted by his keen reason, and scarcely presumed in his prayer. A quiet, peculiar, singsong moment of grace. From a nearby house, he hears "perhaps a voice of some boy or girl, I do not know—singing over and over again, 'Pick it up and read, pick it up and read'" (*Conf* VIII.12.29). He took the child's refrain to "be nothing other than a divine command to open the Book [the Bible] and read the first passage I chanced upon" (*Conf* VIII.12.29). As he hastily looks around for a Bible, he remembers the story of Antony hearing the words of the Gospel of Matthew to leave everything and make a radical choice to follow Christ. Finding the book of Scriptures, Augustine opens to the passage that would be his particular occasion of grace: Paul's Letter to the Romans.

> Not in dissipation and drunkenness, nor in debauchery and lewdness, nor in arguing and jealousy; but put on the Lord Jesus Christ, and make no provision for the flesh or the gratification of your desire. (Romans 13:13-14)

"I had no wish to read further, nor was there need. No sooner had I reached the end of the verse than the light of certainty flooded my heart and all dark shades of doubt fled away" (*Conf* VIII.12.29). In the light of certainty and the strength of conviction, he said, "My face was peaceful now" (*Conf* VIII.12.30). He shares the news with his friend Alypius and his mother Monica.

The story of Augustine's conversion to Christ is not only a story of decision to believe in Christ as the Word Made Flesh. It is not only an intellectual acceptance of Christian teaching—Augustine had in fact come to accept Catholic teaching about Christ months before he could respond in kind to the offer of Divine love. The fullness of conversion incorporates not only mind, but heart and soul. Aided by divine grace, Augustine moved from intellectual acceptance to spiritual surrender and the loving sacrifice it entails. These two acts of a graced will, surrender and sacrifice, are essential dynamics of Augustinian spirituality.

***Surrender.*** The word has two different meanings. There is surrender in the context of a battle or war, of an argument or disagreement. To surrender in such contexts means "to give up" or "to give in." It is to admit defeat under the superior power of physical force or logical argument. It is the white flag that ends a confrontation. On the grand scale of military campaigns, surrenders mark turning points in history. In the humbler annals of our daily lives, it may simply be the best way to bring disagreement to an end and move on.

The second meaning of surrender is different. It is not to give up or give in. It is "to give over." It is the gift of oneself to a beloved. It is the surrender that is love. The story of Augustine's conversion in book eight of *Confessions* is a surrender in love to Love. He gives himself over to God, because he has finally been able to respond to God's love for him in Christ. It is a surrender that brings peace not from the cessation of hostilities, but from a new union in love. The battle had been within Augustine himself, where "two wills fought it out—the old and the new, the one carnal, the other spiritual—and in their struggle tore my soul apart" (*Conf* VIII.5.10). The struggle ends when Augustine surrenders to God, that is, when his will is strengthened by grace and he is able to give himself over to God's love because he feels its attraction and knows its goodness.

In subsequent years, Augustine reflected often and at length on the meaning of love and loving surrender. "What is every love? Does it not consist in the will to become one with the object which it loves; and, when it reaches its object, becomes one with it?" (*Ord* 2.18.48). Love is an inclination, a movement, a longing to become one with the beloved (*Misc 83* XXXV.1). The attraction of the beloved draws us out of ourselves. Without any physical coercion or psychological compulsion, we seek union with the beloved (*Ex Ps* 39.11).

Anyone who has ever "fallen in love" will recognize their experience in Augustine's analysis. *Confessions* is full of the language of love. Augustine knows, of course, that the first flower of romantic love must give way to the long-term growth of maturing love. Our significant relationships—be they romance, friendship, or family love—call us to continual surrender in love over time, a continuous "giving over" of ourselves to the beloved. It is the same when we fall in love with God. In the season of fresh conversion, Augustine tells us how "Childlike, I chattered away to you, my glory, my wealth, my salvation, and my Lord and God" (*Conf* IX.1.1). In the years after writing *Confessions*, Augustine continued to reflect on the love of God even as grace empowered his will to continuous, loving surrender to God.

He notes that through our continuous yielding to God, in and out of season over many years, throughout many trials and difficulties, we become what we love. We slowly become more and more like the God we love, and we share ever more deeply in the divine life of the one who loves us (*Hom 1 Jn* 2.14; Psalm 82:6). Our love increases and becomes more intense, more sure, and more firm (*S* 158.7–9; *Tchg Ch* 1.38.42–39.43). Our movement toward God in love and our union with God in love slowly sanctify us and imperceptibly transform us. We enter into and share in the divine life as we become one with Christ (*Ex Ps* 49.1.2). Graced love is a participation in divine love. God dwells in and amidst our loves and so "we participate in his divinity" (Ex Ps 146.11).

Augustine comments on the poignant language in the First Letter of John: "God is love, and those who abide in love abide in God, and God abides in them" (1 John 4:16). He notes John's successive claims in the letter, successive affirmations that build upon one another to make the connection and seal the identification between God and love. *We are from God. Love is from God. God is Love.* Then, extending John's meaning, Augustine draws his own remarkable conclusion: "*Love is God*—it is God because it is from God" (*Hom 1 Jn* 7.4–6). Our sanctification is immersion in the mystery of love, the Love that made us. The fullness of union with God, our final sanctification in God, the beatific vision, awaits us beyond the mystery of death. But Augustinian spiritual life in this world is a life of love in, for, and with God. It is also a life of love in, for, and with our neighbor—something we will explore in subsequent chapters. Augustine reminds us that while to love God is the first of Jesus' two great commandments, love of neighbor comes first in daily life (*Ser* 265.8.9; *Hom Gos Jn* 17.8). The proof of our love of God is in our loving our neighbors, whom God loves infinitely.

***Sacrifice.*** The mystery of the Incarnation moves beyond the joy of Christmas to include the passion and death of Christ. In book seven of *Confessions* (VII.9.13–14), just after he introduces the idea of the Word Made Flesh, Augustine cites the Christological hymn in Paul's Letter to the Philippians:

> Though he was in the form of God, [Christ Jesus] did not count equality with God a thing to be grasped, but emptied himself, taking the form of a servant, being born in the likeness of men. And being found in human form he humbled himself and became obedient unto death, even death on a cross. (Philippians 2:6-8)

In his assumption of our humanity, the Eternal Word also assumed our fate of death. "Itwas not enough for the only Son of God, co-eternal with the Father, to be born for [us] as a human being from a human being, without his also dying at the hands of the human beings he created" (*S* 218C.1). The "humble God" not only took on our flesh; he took on our death (*S* 218C.4). When preaching to his congregation about the Lord's passion and death, Augustine proclaimed that it was "something incredible, . . . that God has died for the sake of human beings" (*S* 218C.1). "No one has greater love than this, to lay down one's life for one's friends" (John 15:13; *Hom Gos Jn* 84).

God's surrender to us, God's self-donation to us in the Word Made Flesh, God's outpouring of love is total and final in Christ. It is revealed and sealed in Jesus' surrender of his life, his loving self-donation in his death on the cross. When we surrender to God, we enter Jesus' sacrifice and become one with him; our surrender to God immerses us in the mystery of God's sacrifice for us.

If in surrender to Christ we become what we love, then we become one with that which fully expresses God's sacrificial love. If we share ever more deeply in the divine life of the one who loves us, we enter ever more deeply into the cross of Christ. If our union with God in love sanctifies us and transforms us, it is because we have become one with Christ crucified. If graced love is a participation in divine love, it is a sharing in the fullest expression of that love in the death of Jesus. This is what Saint Paul meant when he wrote: "I have been crucified with Christ; it is no longer I who live, but Christ who lives in me; and the life I now live in the flesh I live by faith in the Son of God, who loved me and gave himself for me" (Galatians 2:20). Commenting on Galatians, Augustine wrote, "So Christ lives in the believer by dwelling in the inner person through faith, so that afterwards he may fill him with his vision, when what is mortal is swallowed up by life" (*Com Ep Gal* 17).

The center of Augustinian spirituality is loving relationship with Christ. The heart of that relationship is participation in the blood of Christ, that is, communion with the sacrifice of Christ (1 Corinthians 10:16). The Augustinian spiritual life is one of mystic union with the infinite love of God, lived in the "inner chamber" of our soul where we feel the sweetness of God's love for us and offer a "sacrifice of praise" to the one who sanctifies us (*Conf* IX.4.10; X.34.53).

## Baptism

From earliest New Testament times, conversion to Christ leads to Baptism in Christ. In receiving the Sacrament of Baptism, we profess our faith and celebrate our union with Christ. That, at least, is the sacrament seen from our side, from a human perspective. Just as important, even more important for Augustine, is to see the sacrament from the other side, from the divine perspective. In Baptism, we profess faith, but God professes love. The ritual of Baptism is not only the occasion to express our belief. It is an efficacious expression of God's love for us. To understand how Augustine thought about the Sacrament of Baptism and its place in Christian spirituality, we need to explore the notion of mystery.

***Mystery.*** There are two different understandings of mystery. The first is the kind of mystery that begs to be solved. For example, there are many parts of a jigsaw puzzle that we mix and match and try to fit together to complete the picture. Or, there are hints in a word game or brain teaser that challenge us to sort and search for clues so we can guess the answer or solve the riddle. Or, there are clues hidden amidst the many details of a crime scene, waiting for a detective to uncover them, follow where they lead, and identify the criminal. We love these types of mysteries that challenge our intelligence, test our ability to see patterns, and try our persistence. But it is not mystery in this sense that concerns the sacraments and the spiritual life.

The second type of mystery is different. It is not like a puzzle to be assembled or a problem to be solved. It is not something that can be completed and framed, tucked back in a box, or saved in a virtual file. This second type of mystery does not dissolve under logical scrutiny or submit to algorithms. It remains before us but eludes our comprehension. It draws our attention but escapes our control. It pulls us in like gravity but seems to flout space and time. It can easily overwhelm us, but it cannot destroy us.

There are many examples of this second kind of mystery. When we hold a newborn baby, the mystery of life itself nestles in our arms, overwhelming us with beauty, poignancy, and fragility. When we fall in love, the power of the experience disrupts and decenters our lives. The beloved becomes the focus of our attention and affection, the center of gravity in our personal universe. We may measure the brain chemistry of lovers, but the experience itself bedevils our reason and weakens our knees. A piece of music or a work of art enthralls us with its loveliness or overwhelms us with its force. Its power takes us beyond ourselves into the harmony and complexity of the universe. We feel the "intense beauty of the order of all things" (*Conf* XIII.35.50). At such times when we experience mystery in this second sense, we seem able to touch "that eternal Wisdom who abides above all things" (*Conf* IX.10.25). For Augustine, God the Creator is both hidden in and revealed by all creation. In that sense, he saw the whole of creation as mystery. "The earth, the sea, the sky, and all the creatures in them" are revelatory of the divine (*Ex Ps* 99.5). Reflecting on creation in book eleven of *Confessions*, he wrote,

> Heaven and earth further proclaim that they did not make themselves. "We are because we have been made; we did not exist before we came to be, as though to bring ourselves into being." And their visible existence is the voice with which they say this. It was you who made them, Lord: you are beautiful, so it must have been you, because they are beautiful; you who are good must have made them, because they are good; you who are, because they are. (*Conf* XI.4.6)

***Sacrament.*** Augustine also uses the word mystery in its second sense when speaking about the sacraments. In fact, for Augustine, the words mystery and sacrament are interchangeable. The sacraments of the Church are celebrations of the mystery of our union with Christ, the "mystery, which is Christ in you, the hope of glory" (Colossians 1:27). They proclaim the revelation of God in Christ and our incorporation into the Body of Christ. They are "visible speech" that express invisible mysteries (*L* 55.5.8–9; 7.13; *Ans Faus* 19.16). They make use of simple elements of creation such as water, wine, bread, and oil, as well as human gesture and voice to express the Good News of the Gospel. The Church consecrates these simple things; that is, it makes them holy by using the words of Scripture to invite believers to see and receive the deeper mysteries, which sacraments symbolize and make present for us.

The mystery of God's love revealed in Christ is both hidden in and manifested by the baptismal water and the word of faith that consecrates it. When we celebrate Baptism—our own, our child's, or anyone's—Christ crucified and risen stands before us, reaching out to embrace us in mystical union. The sacrament unites us with him and pulls us into the divine mystery beyond space and time, made present here and now. Speaking to those about to be baptized at an Easter Vigil, Augustine told them that "baptism has the same value as being buried with Christ, as the Apostle says, 'For we are buried together with Christ by baptism into death, that as he was raised from the dead so we also may walk in newness of life' (Romans 6:4)" (*S* 229A.1).

Sacraments are invitations to interiority, to the spiritual life. To celebrate them is to move from the visible to the invisible, from our everyday life to the mystery that dwells within us. Augustinian spirituality does not see the sacraments as obligatory rituals or magical rites designed to attract God's attention. They are opportunities for God to express loving surrender to us, to share sacrificial love for us, to reveal through humble symbols and words the divine will that is always choosing us. In that sense, the sacraments are gifts from God to the Church so that we can together "recall, behold and desire" the God whom we profess by faith (*Trin* XV.5.39), and who is fully present to us and for us in the sacraments.

> The reason these things, brothers and sisters, are called sacraments is that in them one thing is seen, another is to be understood. What can be seen has a bodily appearance, what is to be understood provides spiritual fruit (*S* 272.1).

***Profession.*** In book eight of *Confessions*, as he is leading up to the story of his own conversion, Augustine tells the story of Victorinus (*Conf* VIII.2.5–3.6). He was a famous Roman orator who in his later years converted to Christianity. His spiritual mentor in Rome was the priest Simplicianus, the same priest who later guided Augustine in Milan. Simplicianus told Augustine how Victorinus had confided to him that in his mind and heart he already embraced the Christian faith. Simplicianus replied, "I will not believe that, nor count you among Christians, until I see you in Church" (*Conf*

VIII.2.4). Victorinus responded with the gibe: "It's the walls that make Christians, then?" This situation persisted for a while. It seems that Victorinus feared the taunts of his pagan friends and professional colleagues and did not want to make any public profession of faith. One day, out of the blue, Victorinus approached Simplicianus and requested, "Let's go to the church. I want to become a Christian (*Conf* VIII.2.4)." Simplicianus must have known the story would have an effect on Augustine, who at this point was still wavering. He was certainly aware of parallels between the young Augustine and the old Victorinus, both accomplished Roman rhetoricians.

Augustine ends his account of the story about Victorinus with his own comments about the importance of community. Baptism is not just a personal encounter with Christ. It is an encounter with what Augustine called the Whole Christ. The mystery of Christ's continued presence in the world is through the Church, the community of those united with him in Baptism. For Augustine, the spiritual life is a life lived as a member of the Body of Christ. Augustinian community is not just a social gathering of convenience or conviviality. It is a continuation of the Incarnation among those who have been incorporated into Christ by Baptism. "So if you want to understand the body of Christ, listen to the apostle telling the faithful, 'You, though, are the body of Christ and its members'" (*S* 272; 1 Corinthians 12:27).

Conversion to Christ is not just a matter of Victorinus or Augustine or anyone working out doctrine in their mind and choosing Christ in their heart. Those decisions of mind and will are crucial to the process. However, the fullness of immersion into Christ is communion with all those who have surrendered to him, all those united with his sacrificial love. Augustinian spirituality is a shared spirituality, a sacramental spirituality of communion with the Whole Christ, expressed and effected in Baptism and the other sacraments, especially Eucharist. In cultures that prize individualism over the common good, spirituality is often viewed and practiced as a solitary pursuit within the privacy of one's soul. Augustinian spirituality integrates the interior life with a profound communal dimension. It understands union with God through, with, and in

Christ to involve communion with all those who also believe in Christ and have been baptized.

As Victorinus appeared in the church, professed his faith in Christ, and was baptized, the Body of Christ, that is, "all the people longed to clasp him tenderly to their hearts. And so they did, by loving him and rejoicing with him, for those affections were like clasping hands" (*Conf* VIII.2.5). Let us turn our attention now to the mystery of the Body of Christ.

## Chapter Three

# One Christ Loving Himself

Augustinian spirituality is a spirituality of community and contemplation. The *Monastic Rule* begins, "The main purpose for your having come together is to live harmoniously in your house, intent upon God with one heart and one soul" (*Rule* 1.3). This sentence brings together these two themes of community and contemplation. Community is expressed in the words *come together in your house* and *live harmoniously.* Contemplation is captured in the phrase *with one heart and one soul intent upon God*, or, in Augustine's original Latin, *anima una et cor unum in Deum.* He understood community as shared, intentional, and continuous reflection on the mystery of the divine, moving together toward and into that mystery.

In this chapter, we will explore both community and contemplation and how they shape Augustinian spirituality. First, we will look at Augustine's teaching of the *Totus Christus*, the Whole Christ, in which he expands on Saint Paul's doctrine of the Body of Christ. This idea distinguishes the Augustinian understanding of community by its focus on the abiding presence of Christ in those who are united with him and with each other in his sacrificial love. We will also explore Augustine's approach to contemplation. The members of an Augustinian community are called to support and encourage each other in the daily remembrance of and reflection on the mystery of Christ, who is the source, purpose, and goal of their common life.

## The Body of Christ

When Saint Paul wanted to help Christians understand the meaning of their Baptism, he used an expression that would have been somewhat familiar to them. Other writers in antiquity had also used the image of the human body to express the unity of a group of people. Philosophers, for example, had compared the unity of the city or state to that of the body. We still speak of the "body politic."

Paul, however, forged the analogy in a new way. "You are the Body of Christ." Paul uses this body analogy at least eleven times in his letters (Romans 7:4; 12:4-6; 1 Corinthians 10:16; 12:12; 12:27; Ephesians 3:6; 4:12; 5:23; Colossians 1:18; 1:24; 3:15). With this phrase, the apostle strives to communicate the deepest meaning of Church. Beyond its institutional structures, beyond its doctrines and ethical teachings, beyond its social life and liturgical services, the Church is Christ's Body, and "each of you a member" (1 Corinthians 12:27). He adds, "Each member belongs to all the others" (Romans 12:5).

We could designate Paul's description as an analogy and leave it at that. But he did not write "You are *like* the Body of Christ." He makes an identification. "You *are* the Body of Christ." Perhaps the best way to respect the radical nature of Paul's teaching is to understand it as an analogy that points to a mystery. He uses an arresting analogy to direct our attention to a profound mystery. It is a mystery in the second sense of that word, that is, a reality we can acknowledge but never fully understand or totally comprehend.

Pope Pius XII invited the Church to reflect on Paul's teaching in his 1943 Encyclical *The Mystical Body of Christ.* Amidst the carnage of World War II, Pius called the faithful to reflect on the deepest meaning of their identity as Christians. He drew from Paul's theology of the Body of Christ to call for charity and forgiveness in a world dismembered by violence. Pius pleaded for Christians to remember that their common Baptism into Christ transcended the painful divisions among nations, cultures, and political agendas. He also acknowledged the mysterious nature of this spiritual reality:

> We are not ignorant of the fact that this profound truth of our union with the Divine Redeemer . . . is shrouded in darkness by a veil that impedes our power to understand and explain it, both because of the hidden nature of the doctrine itself, and of the limitations of our human intellect. (*The Mystical Body of Christ* no. 78)

In this encyclical, Pope Pius cites Augustine eleven times. He mentions how Augustine elaborated and expanded Paul's teaching of the Body of Christ with the idea of the Whole Christ (*The Mystical Body of Christ* no. 67). With that phrase, the pope suggests, Augustine opened deeper dimensions of Paul's theology.

## Totus Christus—The Whole Christ

Two important teachings in the Pauline letters are foundation stones for Augustinian spirituality. One is Paul's teaching about God's grace, unmerited but freely given. We have seen how important grace is for Augustinian spirituality and its discernment of God's presence within our minds and hearts amidst the challenges of life. The second Pauline teaching essential to Augustinian spirituality is the Body of Christ.

These two Pauline teachings come together in one of Augustine's homilies on the Gospel of John. Augustine was preaching on John 5:20-23, where the Gospel reflects on the intimate relationship between God the Father and God the Son. Augustine moves deftly from the relationship between Father and Son to the relationship between the Son and the congregation he was addressing:

> Let's congratulate ourselves and give thanks for having been made not only Christians, but Christ. Do you understand, brothers and sisters, the grace of God upon us; do you grasp that? Be filled with wonder, rejoice and be glad; we have been made

> Christ. For if he is the head, and we the members, then he and we are the whole man. (*Hom Gos Jn* 21.8)

He then goes on in the same homily to quote Saint Paul on "the fullness of Christ" in his members (Ephesians 4:13) and Paul's proclamation, "Now you are the Body of Christ" (1 Corinthians 2:27). Augustine's rhetoric becomes graphic in his desire to have his people understand their unity with Christ. He goes so far as to say that Christ continues to learn in and through us, just as Christ continues to suffer when we suffer:

> Because we too are members of the Son,
> and it is as if he is learning
> in his members what we are learning
> as his members.
> In what way is he learning in us?
> In the same way as he is suffering in us.
> How do we prove he is suffering in us?
> From that voice from heaven,
> *Saul, Saul, why are you persecuting me?*
> (Acts 9:4; *Hom Gos Jn* 21.7)

Augustine finds the fullest expression of the union between Christians and Christ, as Paul had, in the Sacrament of the Eucharist. He reminds his congregation that the Eucharistic bread and wine become the Body and Blood of Christ. "What you see here on the table of the Lord is bread and wine; but this bread and wine, when the word is applied to it, becomes the body and blood of *the* Word, . . . for 'the Word became flesh and dwelt among us'" (John 1:14; *S* 229.1–2). But he has more to say about the Eucharist. Augustine tells us not to stop with the change in the bread and wine on the altar. We must move from the change on the altar to the change in the congregation, to the change in us. "In this sacrament Christ presents us his own body and blood—and, what's more, this is what he makes us into, what our very selves become" (*S* 229.1–2).

Augustine affirms that the transformation (what later theologians would call the transubstantiation) occurs not only on the altar, in the bread and wine. We who believe are also transformed into the Body of Christ. The reality of Christ's Body is both on the altar and throughout the congregation. "So if it's you that are the body of Christ and his members, the mystery means that you have been placed on the Lord's table; what you receive is the mystery that means you" (*S* 272.1).

The divine creative act at the very heart of Eucharist effects transformation not only in the bread and wine, but also in us who receive Holy Communion. The Eucharist is the sacrament of unity: of our unity with the loving sacrifice and risen life of Christ; and of our unity with each other as members of Christ's Body.

Augustine has still more to tell us. The Eucharist, he explains, is also a reminder, a celebration of our unity with all members of the Body of Christ around the world and throughout history. Listen to how Augustine expands the meaning of the Body of Christ:

> All of us together are the members of Christ and his body; *not only* those of us who are in this place, but throughout the whole world; and *not only* those of us who are alive at this time, but what shall I say? From Abel the just right up to the end of the world, as long as people beget and are begotten, *any of the just* who make the passage through this life, all who live now, all that will be born after us, all constitute the one body of Christ, while they are each individually members of Christ. (*S* 314.11)

This is Augustine's teaching of the Whole Christ, the *Totus Christus*. It is his powerful extension of Paul's theology of the Body of Christ. The Body of the Risen Christ transcends time and space; it extends around the world and across centuries. We are all united with the Risen Christ—all peoples of all time who have heard the Gospel and believe in Christ, and, he adds, *all the just*—more on that later, for he seems to reach beyond the baptized.

As we have seen, the waters of Baptism both reveal and conceal the power of God who incorporates us into the sacrificial love of Christ to make us members of his Body. In the same sacramental way, the Eucharistic bread and wine both reveal and conceal our communion with Christ and with one another. The Eucharistic symbols are "visible speech," commemorating God's promise of a New Covenant, expressing God's passionate commitment to us, making present the Word Made Flesh, who is now one with our flesh. To partake of the bread and wine is to realize, express, and celebrate the mystery of our communion with the cross, with the sacrificial love of Christ, with the resurrection of Christ from the dead:

> When you receive the body of Christ, it is to what you are that you reply Amen, and by so replying you express assent. What you hear, what you see is: The Body of Christ, and you answer Amen. So be a member of the Body of Christ, in order to make that Amen true. (*S* 272.1)

Augustinian spirituality is a Eucharistic spirituality. The Sacrament of the Eucharist reveals and conceals the spiritual source of Augustinian community. Indeed, it is a sacramental sign of that community. "O sacrament of piety! O sign of unity! O bond of charity! Whoever wants to live has something to live on. Let them approach. Let them believe. Let them belong to the body so as to be given life" (*Hom Gos Jn* 26:13–14).

## Contemplation

The Augustinian college where I taught for many years offered weekly adoration of the Blessed Sacrament in one of the chapels on campus. This provided students with an opportunity for quiet reflection and prayer. One evening, I visited the chapel and found several students praying in the Eucharistic presence. What surprised me was that some of them were members of the small group of

Evangelical Protestant students on the campus. Finding Evangelicals praying before the Blessed Sacrament presented in a very Catholic monstrance aroused my curiosity.

Over the next few days, I managed to ask these students about their presence at the Catholic practice of adoration. Their response was intriguing. "We need a place where we don't have to answer texts or messages, where we can turn our phones off, where we can find peace and quiet, and no one can disturb us; we find this place in the weekly adoration." It was not the time to go into differences between Catholic and Protestant understandings of the Eucharist. But it was an opportunity to affirm their search for peace, for quiet, for contemplation. In his *Monastic Rule*, Augustine writes about the chapel or oratory in the community:

> In the prayer room, no one should do anything other than that for which it is intended; that's why we call it a prayer room. So if someone wants to pray there during their free time, even outside the appointed hours, they are free to so do, and are not hindered by someone using that space for some other business. (*Rule* II.11)

These young, faithful Christian students needed a protected space where they could devote some of their free time to prayer, "unhindered" by the business or busyness of anyone else. Their response to my question expressed their need for time to listen to their restless hearts and time to listen to God. Like other young adults, like all of us, they live in a world where finding space for prayer is a challenge, a world where contemplation is countercultural.

We might imagine that Augustine's world, the fourth and fifth-century world of the late Roman Empire, was much quieter than our time. But Augustine's directive in the *Rule* that no one use prayer space "for some other business" signals that even a world without the internet and social media could be noisy and busy, beset with distraction, disturbed by "other business" or, as Augustine's Latin expresses it, *aliquid agendum*—another agenda.

The *Monastic Rule* is not the only place where Augustine addresses the importance of prayer. He encourages the layfolk in his congregation to allot time and space for prayer, for silent interior reflection:

> Let's leave time for reflection. Let's generously allow something also to silence. Return to yourself. Withdraw from all the din. Look inside yourself. See if you find there any pleasant, private nook in your consciousness where you don't rehearse an argument, where you don't grow litigious and prepare your case, where you don't brood over pig-headed quarrels. Be gentle in hearing the Word, in order to understand. (*S* 52.22)

We can distinguish three Augustinian understandings of prayer that enrich the spiritual life, three kinds of prayer for which the community should provide its members time, space, and encouragement. These three can be described as follows: prayer as desire; meditation as interpretation; and mystical union as dwelling in the divine presence. These are not three iron-clad distinctions that never overlap. Rather, they express three different modes of prayer which can interpenetrate and intensify each other, three ways of being in God's presence with the desire to hear the Divine Word, the Word Made Flesh.

***Prayer as Desire.*** In the year 411, Augustine received a letter from a very wealthy Roman widow by the name of Proba. She was living near Hippo, having escaped to North Africa from the sack of Rome in 410. In her letter, Proba asked Augustine about Saint Paul's instruction to "pray always" (1 Thessalonians 5:17). He responded at length with *Letter 130*, which is really a short book on the nature of Christian prayer. Among the many insights into prayer that Augustine offers to Proba are his thoughts on prayer as desire.

The urge to pray is as natural as our desire to be happy. We instinctively align our desire to be happy with appeals to God to secure that happiness. As her bishop, Augustine counsels Proba that true happiness lies in union with God in Christ, which reaches fullness in eternal life. In the meantime, God knows what we need in this life, even before we ask (Matthew 6:8). In fact, the purpose of our prayer is not to inform God about our doings and longings, which God already knows quite well, but to open our hearts so that we can receive what God longs to give us:

> God does not want our will, which he cannot fail to know, to become known to him, but our desire, by which we can receive what he prepares to give, to be exercised in prayers. For what he prepares to give is very great, but we are very small and narrow for receiving it. (*L* 130.8.17)

Prayer is not a matter of naming our needs and negotiating with God. It is a matter of expressing our desire, sharing our want, acknowledging our longing, admitting our distress. This is the sacrifice God wants from us: simply the yearning of our restless heart. Offer God your hunger; God takes care of the rest. So we can pray simply by sharing our desire with God.

Referring to the desert Christians in the East, Augustine suggests to Proba that she pray like the "brothers in Egypt" who "are said to say frequent prayers, but very short ones that are tossed off as if in a rush" (*L* 130.10.20). Or, we can spend longer periods of prayer, so long as we realize that multiplying words is not necessary. "Much talking is one thing: a lasting love is another" (*L* 130.10.19). In addition to these short, occasional prayers throughout the day, the regular times for prayer each morning, evening, and night will also deepen our desire and so mature our prayer:

> But at certain hours and moments we also pray to God in words so that by those signs of things we may admonish ourselves, realize how much we have advanced in this desire, and arouse ourselves more intensely to increase it. For a more worthy result ensues when a more fervent love has preceded. (*L* 130.9.18)

Offering God our desire allows God to direct or redirect it. Praying this way allows grace to purify and redeem all our desires, to align them with true happiness. So often our desires, even those we bring to prayer, are confused and uncertain, even conflicting. This should not be cause for discouragement. "Likewise the Spirit helps us in our weakness; for we do not know how to pray as we ought, but the Spirit himself intercedes for us with sighs too deep for words" (Romans 8:26). The Spirit of God, as Paul writes in Romans, joins us in prayer and supplies our intent. The Holy Spirit is divine desire that becomes one with our desires to redeem and purify them, so that we can advance in an authentic desire for true happiness, "and arouse ourselves more intensely to increase it" (*L* 130.9.18). Our desire to pray is itself prayer. Augustine calls it the prayer that never ceases:

> But there is another kind of prayer that never ceases, an interior prayer that is desire. Whatever else you may be engaged upon, if you are all the while desiring that Sabbath, you never cease to pray. If you do not want to interrupt your prayer, let your desire be uninterrupted. Your continuous desire is your continuous voice. You will only fall silent if you stop loving. (*Ex Ps* 37.17)

***Prayer as Meditation.*** The last sentence in the earlier quotation from *Sermon* 52, "Be gentle in hearing the Word, in order to understand," provides another perspective on Augustine's understanding of prayer. It shows how he thought about prayer as meditation.

Christian prayer draws inspiration and language from Scripture. Both Testaments, Old and New, are the inspired Word of God, received in faith and reverence from our forebearers in faith. When he was unexpectedly called to serve as priest, while visiting the city of Hippo, Augustine asked the bishop who ordained him if he could return home for a time to prepare for his ministry. He wanted particularly time for prayerful study of the Bible.

For Augustine, Christian prayer is intimately bound with Sacred Scripture. Prayerful engagement with Scripture moves in two directions: inward and outward. The first movement is inward, into the text. It is the desire to understand the meaning of the text in itself. At the beginning of book eleven of *Confessions*, Augustine includes a prayer that God will help him understand the book of Genesis, which he is about to explore and explain to his readers. He compares Scripture to a vast forest, with many "pages deep in shadow, obscure in their secrets," where he desires to "roam and browse, lie down and ruminate" (*Conf* XI.2.3). He confesses his longing to understand and interpret the text correctly, so "that I find grace before you, so that the inner meaning of your words may be opened to me as I knock at their door" (*Conf* XI.2.4). It is a prayer for divine guidance amidst the mystery of the Word Made Flesh as revealed in sacred text.

Augustine's book *Teaching Christianity* is a guide for preachers who strive to invite people into the sacred text to learn its teachings and prayerfully meditate on its mysteries. He stresses the importance of learning about the language and culture from which the text arose. But he moves from the facts of history, geography, and linguistics to the challenge of meaning. How should one interpret the sacred text? In discussing the differences between reading a text literally and reading it figuratively, Augustine directs that any figurative interpretation should be judged by the rule of love. In reading Scripture,

> Love reigns supreme with its just laws of loving God for God's sake, and oneself and one's neighbor for God's sake. So this rule will be observed in dealing with figurative expressions, that you should take pains to turn over and over in your mind what you read, until your interpretation of it is led right through to the kingdom of charity. (*Tchg Ch* III.15.23)

Love, then, is *the* principle of interpretation, the guide for discerning the meaning of sacred text, be it the meaning intended by the author, the meaning received by the original community for whom it was written, or the meanings discovered and discerned by communities of faith in subsequent times and other places (*Conf* III.7.14).

The second direction of interpretation of Scripture is outward, that is, the text turned toward us, toward how we appropriate it for our lives. How does the text speak to us about how to live? How does it enrich our spirituality? *Confessions* is Augustine's long, prayerful conversation with God. All throughout, he uses Sacred Scripture to gain insight into the meaning of his life in light of his faith. *Confessions* models how to hold up our lives to the mirror of Sacred Scripture. We bring our restless desires, our persistent questions, our tentative decisions, or failed resolve and surrender it all to the Word of God revealed in the sacred text. This is not a search for one-to-one correspondence between what's happening in our life and a specific text from the Bible. Prayerful meditation is not a matter of mystery in the first sense of piecemeal puzzle or logical problem, where we match Bible texts to events.

Rather, it is surrender to the mysterious dimensions of who we have been, who we are, and who we hope to become in light of God's Word. It is quiet attention to the desires and needs that we feel within us, confessing they are part of us even though we may not understand them. It is admission that responsibility for what we have done often feels like it may overwhelm us. It is keen awareness of the beauty, poignancy, and fragility of the life that is God's gift, the fullness of which we understand only in the light of our faith. It is bringing the mystery of our self, our soul, to the mystery of God who speaks to us through the texts of Sacred Scripture. "Deep calls unto deep at the thunder of your cataracts; all your waves and your billows have gone over me" (Psalm 42:7).

The rule for the outward direction of Scripture, for using the text to interpret our lives, for seeking meaning in the text for our spirituality, is the same as for seeking to understand the text in itself. It is the rule of love. Prayer as meditation is to approach

Scripture with the desire to understand how the infinite love of God is operative in our lives. In one sense, the whole of Augustine's *Confessions* is prayer as meditation. He shows us how to bring passages from Scripture to the events of our lives so that Scripture comes alive for us, and at the same time, our lives come to new significance in the light of Scripture. In prayerful meditation, we turn over and over in our minds what we read in Scripture until we find an interpretation of the text that deepens our love for God, our self, and our neighbor (*Tchg Ch* III.15.23).

There is another dimension of Augustinian prayer as meditation, a sacramental dimension. We can read and reflect on Sacred Scripture to receive graced enlightenment and empowerment for our lives. We can also reflect on the "visible speech," the visible Word of God that are the sacraments. Augustinian prayer as meditation is not only scriptural. It is also sacramental. The symbols, rituals, and words of sacraments offer another source of inspiration. We can turn prayerfully to the sacraments to encounter the presence of God among us. We find in the sacraments, especially in the daily celebration of the Eucharist, meaning and purpose for our spiritual lives.

When we celebrate Eucharist, we offer our desires, our questions, our restlessness, our successes, and our failures in union with the sacrifice of Christ. In the prayerful celebration of the Mass, we surrender our lives in their fullness and complexity to God, who transforms them into "an acceptable sacrifice" and thereby gives them new meaning. Communion with God in the Body of Christ bestows that new meaning to all we are and all we do. Our lives, our souls, our bodies are transformed, transubstantiated if you will, by the Holy Spirit, who breathes over and within us "with sighs too deep for words" (Romans 8:26). The Mass joins reflection on Scripture in the Liturgy of the Word to reflection on sacrament in the Liturgy of the Eucharist. Both Word and Eucharist are invitations to meditative prayer, in which we bring our lives to God for renewal and transformation.

***Prayer as Mystical Union.*** Among the different spiritual traditions in Christianity, we can find different understandings of mystical union. It is often described as a special kind of prayer that is simple and unitary, beyond language and adequate description, and different from meditation, which is discursive and imaginative. Some spiritual writers also examine the theme of holy desire as part of mystical prayer. We find such themes in the writings of Saint Theresa of Avila, in her theology of contemplation.

We have already seen that Augustine's pursuit of Neoplatonic spirituality left him with the powerful memory of two different mystical encounters with "light incomparable," with the transcendent and unitary *That Which Is.* Augustine also tells us, in book nine, about another such experience. It was the mystical experience he and his mother, Monica, shared shortly before her death at Ostia during the journey back to Africa. However, he describes this occurrence differently. It occurred after his conversion and Baptism, and so reflects the integration of Christian faith and mysticism. Their shared mystical ascent, that "step by step traversed all bodily creatures and heaven itself," was inspired not by philosophy, but by faith in the Eternal Wisdom of God who made all things that are and "have ever been or ever will be." Monica and Augustine's mystical encounter with God is not a solitary metaphysical search, but a shared, loving embrace mediated by "your Word, our Lord, who . . . renews all things," and who met them "unmediated" by creation or any creature. The experience was a brief "passing moment that left us aching for more" (*Conf* IX.10.24).

Such mystical prayer continued to be part of Augustine's spiritual life, though intermittently. He tells us in book ten, "From time to time you lead me into an inward experience quite unlike any other, a sweetness beyond understanding" (*Conf* X.40.65). He describes these experiences as being intense glimpses of a future where "my life will not be what it is now, though what it will be I cannot tell." He seeks through poetry to describe these mystical encounters with the divine:

> You called, shouted, broke through my deafness;
> you flared, blazed, banished my blindness;
> you lavished your fragrance, I gasped,

and now I pant for you;
I tasted you, and I hunger and thirst;
you touched me, and I burned for
your peace. (*Conf* X.27.38)

As noted above, these three kinds of prayer—desire, meditation, and mystical union—are not totally distinct and discrete. In the spiritual life, they more often than not penetrate each other. As we bring our desires into prayer, they often become dimensions of our meditations on the Word of God and part of our celebration of the sacraments. Meditation on Word and sacrament, in turn, can become the occasion for a mystical experience, during which we feel, see, or hear different, manifold aspects of the mystery of our union with the *Totus Christus*—the Whole Christ, and so with the divine itself.

An Augustinian understanding of mystical union refers not only to precious moments of ecstasy that might grace our prayer from time to time. Augustinian mysticism includes, welcomes, and embraces our human desires, because Augustine knew that in moments of mystical union our desire meets God's desire and the two become one love, "One Christ loving himself" (*Hom 1 Jn* 10.3). Mystical union emerges from and returns to our meditation on Word and sacrament. Meditative prayer, in turn, augments and purifies our desire. Such prayer widens and deepens our souls to receive more and more of the gift of divine self-donation.

## Community and Contemplation

The motto on Pope Leo XIV's coat of arms, *In Illo Uno Unum*, is taken from Saint Augustine's commentary on Psalm 127. "We who are many are *one in him, who is one—nos multi in illo uno unum*" (*Ex Ps* 127.3). In his long exposition of this psalm, Augustine spends many paragraphs reflecting on the tension, we might even call it the paradox, the seeming contradiction between being many and yet one. The global community of Christians is wonderfully diverse by virtue of the different histories, languages, and cultures that comprise it, as well as by the different denominations and ecclesial rites. At the same time and amidst such differences, Augustine, echoing Paul, claims that all Christians are one in Christ by their baptismal incorporation into the Body of Christ. "All Christians, in union with their head who has ascended into heaven, form one Christ. It is not as though he were one and we many; no, we who are many are one in him, who is one" (*Ex Ps* 127.3).

Augustinian spirituality is a loving embrace of "the many" within the mystery of "the one." It aspires to a hospitable welcome that honors difference and, at the same time, seeks to live a common life based on the truth of our union in Christ. Yet our experience tells us that difference all too easily becomes division. Communities can all too easily lose their cohesion. Distinct personalities, peculiar habits, familial backgrounds, cultural expectations, educational disparities, and so many other factors threaten to break apart a life lived in common so that it becomes a life lived in separate condos. Communities, be they gathered in monasteries, friaries, or convents, or dispersed among lay confraternities, third orders, and societies, can fall apart under the centrifugal forces of pride that defile and demean difference. Augustine knew this very well from his own experience of living in community. After stating the ideal of common life at the beginning of his *Monastic Rule*, he spends most of the subsequent chapters giving advice about how to negotiate difference. The next three chapters that follow in this book also will attend to difference by studying how to cultivate the virtues necessary for life in community.

For Augustine, being "intent upon God" is essential to community. Prayer as desire, as meditation, and as mystical union is what reveals the unity, the communion that supports and ennobles difference. Prayer, in all its forms, taps the hidden waters of our unity in Christ to refresh and strengthen our common life. We can *come together* and *live harmoniously* only because we do so *with one heart and one soul intent upon God.* Immersed in the mysteries of prayerful desire, meditation, and mystical union, we can look at our brother or sister and accept them, forgive them, encourage them. No matter how different they may be from us, no matter how disturbing or disruptive that difference may sometimes feel, no matter the force of the conflicting desires that arise out of difference, we can bring it all to our contemplation and meditate on Christ's prayer for all his many members: "For them do I sanctify myself, since they themselves, too, are myself" (*Hom Gos Jn* 108.5; John 17:19).

# Part Two

## Participation

Augustinian spirituality arises from the mysteries of faith, from union with God and communion with one another through, with, and in Christ. It also draws from centuries of wisdom, of how to participate in communities inspired by the gift of God's love for us and Christ's commandment to love one another.

Part two looks at practice, at the personal and communal dynamics that comprise Augustinian spiritual life. These include the habits and virtues that grace shapes and forms within us so that we can live the "good life" of those who cherish community and who "live in freedom under grace" (*Rule* VIII.48).

O Lord my God, hear my prayer,
may your mercy hearken to my longing,
a longing on fire not for myself alone,
but to serve the ones I dearly love.

*Confessions* XI.2.3

Domine Deus meus, intende orationi meae,
et misericordia tua exaudiat desiderium meum,
quoniam non mihi soli aestuat,
sed usui vult esse fraternae caritati.

# Chapter Four

# Listening, Interiority, Memory

In part one, we examined the foundations of Augustinian spirituality: the mystery of the Incarnation, graced conversion to Christ who dwells within us, and contemplation of our communion with God and one another. While we cannot comprehend the depth of these mysteries of faith, they are at the heart of Augustinian spirituality and community. They call us to reflect on their meaning for our lives in the light of Scripture and in the celebration of sacrament.

Augustinian spirituality, however, also attends to the practical side of living the spiritual life. It seeks ways of living together that disclose the mystery of our union with Christ, and our communion with one another. Augustine often insisted that when it comes to the two great commandments to love God and our neighbor, the mystery of the love of God has priority (Matthew 22:36-40; Mark 12:28-34). However, love of neighbor comes first in daily life (*S* 265.8.9):

> In terms of precept, the love of God comes first; but, in terms of practice, the love of neighbor comes first. . . . So, then, love your neighbor, and contemplate in yourself the source of your loving your neighbor; there, as best you can, you will see God. Begin, therefore, by loving your neighbor. (*Hom Gos Jn* 17.8)

One of the ways to love our neighbor is to listen.

## Listening

One of the greatest gifts we can give a child is to listen. When we listen to a toddler or teenager who is expressing a feeling or a need, our attentiveness affirms them. To put everything else aside and signal our interest by word and gesture is an act of love. Augustine understood love to be an inclination, a movement, or a striving to become one with the beloved (*Misc 83* XXXV.1). When we sit down to listen more carefully to a little one who wants our ear, our movement is not only a change of posture. It is a movement of mind and heart. Our love draws us out of our own present concerns and worries and impels us to enter the world of the one who needs our consideration at that moment. Our care for them urges us to become one with them by entering as best we can into their sphere of experience and understanding, to discover what has prompted them to approach us (*Ex Ps* 39.11).

In his book about teachers and students, *Instructing Beginners in Faith*, Augustine presents an idea that has been described as co-inhabitation. It helps us to understand the power of true listening. He writes that when teachers and students listen carefully to each other they "live within each other" (*Instr Bg* 12.17). He encourages teachers to listen to their students with the love of a father, a mother, a sibling, in order to be "united with them in heart." Listening is an act of love that strengthens children, and, in turn, tutors them in how to love and listen to others.

Of course, it is no different for adults. We all want to be listened to. When our particular world is fraught with troublesome questions or disturbed by unruly desires, or when we feel overwhelmed by decisions that lay before us, nothing is so empowering and so liberating as another human being who puts their own agenda aside and turns their attention solely to what we struggle to share. We hear Augustine expressing this hope in *Confessions*. He wants his readers to "lay their ears to his heart" so that they can come to know who he really is (*Conf* X.3.4). Like anyone who takes the risk of opening up, he expresses worry about those who think they know him, the listeners, or readers "who know me without really knowing me" (*Conf* X.3.4).

***Listening in the Rule.*** Augustine begins his *Monastic Rule* by recalling the double commandment to love God and one another. He exhorts members of the community to live together harmoniously and to be of one mind and heart intent upon God (*Rule* I.3). He then spends all the remaining paragraphs of chapter one addressing a problem that must have been common in these small communities. Some came to the monastery from the poorest strata of society, from conditions of poverty, and little or no social standing. Others left behind significant social rank and prosperity. These communities of men and women, comprised of people coming together from very different backgrounds, seem to have found it difficult at times "to live harmoniously."

In addressing this tension, Augustine suggests that pride could be at work underneath community problems related to social status. It may be the pride of the rich, boasting about giving up so much from their past life. Or, it may be the pride of those who were once poor and now boast of their newfound association with people of importance. In either case, pride can scuttle the whole reason for their having come together (*Rule* I.5–9).

Throughout the rest of the chapters in the *Rule*, Augustine gives advice on how to address many other differences found in these voluntary communities of spiritual seekers. As we have seen, people have different prayer habits and practices. So Augustine talks about respecting the purpose of the chapel or prayer room. In addition, there are different degrees of physical strength and fitness among members of the community, as well as bouts of sickness that at times require special care and dispensation from monastic practice. He urges attention to these different conditions and needs. Sexual temptation may be stronger for some members and so require vigilance. Some people need more in the line of food, clothing, and bedding, while others can be more sparing in their use of such things.

Augustine wants members of the community to become aware of the many different needs and conditions in their midst. He wants people to notice and carefully consider each other's necessity, to discern various circumstances and respond judiciously. In short, he wants them to listen to each other. Only then can they respond with loving care. Borrowing his language from *Confessions*, we can say that he encourages members of the community to "lay their ears to each other's hearts" so that they can "really know" each other and take care of one another. As expressed in the formation program of the Augustinian contemplative nuns: "It is therefore essential to initiate and support training processes that foster the opening of the heart and mind to humble, profound and attentive listening" (*Ratio Formationis*, Augustinian Nuns 4.3.2. no.144).

***Graced Listening.*** Listening to each other in ways that help us "really know" one another is not easy. It is challenging to put aside our own perspective and preference in order to attend to another person. It is arduous to refrain from judgment and enter empathically into the world of another, especially when their background and experience is very different from one's own. Augustine once began a sermon by asking his congregation to be still and listen to him: "Do not have your hearts in your ears, but ears in your hearts" (*S* 380.1). We might paraphrase his request this way: "Don't let all of the concerns troubling your heart impair your hearing; rather, listen with all your heart." No matter how you describe it, listening can be difficult. As the Augustinian nuns advise, it takes training.

Pride can prevent us from listening. Pride prioritizes the satisfaction of the self over the needs of the neighbor. It strives to maintain control and so resists relinquishing one's own agenda, a surrender that effective listening requires. Pride can keep us ignorant of what the other person is trying to say, stoking our resistance with self-concern, rendering us deaf. It can also weaken our resolve and enervate our will, so that we remain emotionally paralyzed when someone tries to share their thoughts, feelings, or needs with us.

To listen well not only requires training. It requires grace. The psalmist speaks of God's attentiveness to us: "Even before a word is on my tongue, O Lord, you know it completely" (Psalm 139:4). In commenting on this psalm (which was numbered Psalm 138 in the Latin Psalter he used), Augustine compares God to the Father in the parable of the Prodigal Son, whose parental love impels him to run out, meet, and embrace the prodigal who is still making his way home (Luke 15:11-32). Even from afar, the Father knows what is in the repentant mind and homesick heart of his son. "My mind is already an open book to you," writes Augustine, using the words of the psalm to put himself in the shoes of the prodigal son, and to imagine what the youth experienced as he saw his father approaching (*Ex Ps* 138.5). "He had understood the boy's thoughts even when he was far away" (*Ex Ps* 138.5). God is the eternal listener with infinite patience, the One who always hears us, even when we ourselves cannot articulate what we think, feel, or need.

We are loved and listened to by God. Contemplation on this mystery of our faith is what, in turn, transforms us into loving listeners. The love of God for us helps us to love one another by listening to each other as God has listened to us. Divine grace helps us prioritize the second commandment to love one another as God has loved us. In addition, God's grace enlightens our minds and strengthens our will so that we can effectively put aside our concerns and listen with open minds and loving hearts to those around us.

A powerful image of the attentive Christian transformed by listening is that of the apostle John at the Last Supper. The Gospel describes him as reclining next to Jesus, intimately listening to the Word Made Flesh (John 13:23-25). Commenting on this passage, Augustine paints a picture of the beloved disciple resting his head on the breast of Jesus so that he could hear the heartbeat of God, so he could feel the breath of God, so he could drink in the mystery of the Eternal Word. Augustine wrote, "From that breast he drank in secret; but what he drank in secret, he proclaimed openly, so that all nations might learn . . . that Jesus was the only Son of the Father, the Word of the Father, coeternal with the one who begot him" (*Hom Gos Jn* 36.1). John becomes a symbol of what we all can be. By listening to Jesus, we hear the mystery of the depth of divine love for each of us. Like John, when we listen to the Word of God and share in the sacrament of the Lord's Supper, we, in turn, become graced listeners and occasions of grace for those who come to us seeking our communion with their concerns.

Listening, then, is at the heart of Augustinian spirituality: listening to Christ in the Word of Scripture and in his sacramental presence, especially in the Eucharist. Listening is also at the heart of Augustinian community: listening to one another just as God, the loving Father, listens to us and understands our thoughts, no matter how "far away" we may feel. Divine grace reveals God's loving attention to us. That same grace enlightens and empowers us to listen to our brothers and sisters, "so that we may be able to console those who are in any affliction with the consolation with which we ourselves are consoled by God" (2 Corinthians 1:4).

## Interiority

The image of a God who listens intimately to us, who rests the divine ear on our human heart, is found throughout Augustine's writings. The divine presence awaits us in prayer. So, Augustine counsels, go within to meet God. This turn to interiority is one of the most important themes in *Confessions* and in Augustinian spirituality. The abiding truth of the Incarnation is that the Eternal Word Made Flesh dwells within us, in the depths of our soul. God is "more intimately present to me than my innermost being" (*Conf* III.6.11).

Augustine admits, however, that he spent many years of his young life looking for happiness outside himself, deaf to the whispers within his soul. Interiority came to him only at the time of his conversion in his early thirties.

Late have I loved you,<br>
Beauty so ancient and so new,<br>
late have I loved you!<br>
Lo, you were within,<br>
but I outside,<br>
seeking there for you,<br>
and upon the shapely things<br>
you have made<br>
I rushed headlong, I, misshapen.<br>
You were with me,<br>
but I was not with you.<br>
(*Conf* X.27.38)

For Augustine, conversion to Christ was a call to go within, an invitation to return to himself, a summons to listen to his soul. One of Augustine's earliest books was entitled *True Religion.* He wrote it shortly after his return to Africa while still living in the little community he founded in his home town of Thagaste. He introduces the importance of interiority for the spiritual life of a Christian. Augustine, the recent convert, urges his friends, "Do not go outside, come back into yourself. It is in the inner self that Truth dwells" (*Tr Rel* 39.72). A few years later, after he was ordained, he wrote to his friend Nebridius about the importance of making time for interiority. Amidst the demands of his ministry and the desire to spend time with friends both near and far, Augustine insists on the importance of "careful repose," that is, time and space to dwell quietly with God in the "sanctuary of the mind" away from the "uproar and restless comings and goings" of daily life (*L* 10.2–3).

When the Order of Saint Augustine was founded in the thirteenth century, it received and embraced Augustine's counsel of interiority. The *Constitutions* of the Order state,

> By way of the interior life we are made capable of knowing and loving him, and we share in his life. It is necessary, then, that we always turn back to ourselves, and entering within, diligently work toward perfecting our heart so that, praying with uninterrupted desire we may come to God (*Constitutions of the Order of Saint Augustine* I.II.23)

Augustinian communities live among and minister to the People of God, even while spiritual interiority remains at the center of their religious life. Contemplation needs to be "understood, respected and accepted as a component of Augustinian tradition" (*Constitutions* I.I.5). For all who wish to live an Augustinian spiritual life, professed religious as well as lay people in their various circumstances, "holy leisure" is essential, finding time and making space for spiritual interiority (*L* 220.3). Amidst all our responsibilities and the demands put on us by others, even those we care for, we need also to provide for what we "love and long for," that is, contemplation within the interior sanctuary of our soul (*L* 5.1). There, in the inner cloister of our soul, we plead "Let me know myself, let me know you: this is my prayer" (*Sol* II.1.1).

***Asceticism.*** Asceticism is a common part of the spiritual life in most traditions. It usually refers to different kinds of self-discipline that keep our five senses disciplined and under control, so that they do not deter us from our spiritual path. In book ten of *Confessions*, in the midst of his reflections on memory, Augustine talks about the need for asceticism with regard to the senses. His concern is that our senses can leave us living on the surface of life with "only the externals." Our senses, though beautiful in themselves and the means by which we receive the beauty of God's creation, can nonetheless distract us from "true insight" into our interior life and from the divine presence in our souls (*Conf* X.34.52). He advises that we need to be diligent and balanced in how we respect and respond to our senses, appreciating their beauty, but not allowing unruly desires to disrupt love of God and neighbor.

A balanced, healthy asceticism protects the time, space, and predisposition necessary for prayer. But no matter how diligent our asceticism, responsibilities make demands on our time and energy. Augustine himself, as a busy older bishop, complained about the amount of work that kept him up at night:

> If I could give you an account of all my days and wakeful nights expended on other indispensable tasks, you would be saddened and astonished at the number of matters that bother me and simply cannot be deferred, and prevent my doing what you ask of me . . . so many urgent things to dictate, matters which cannot be put off. (*L* 139.3)

Once, when writing to a group of monks, he expressed envy of their quiet, contemplative life. He tells them he would much prefer to work quietly in the garden than to deal with other people's squabbles, arguments, and grievances, which took so much of his time each day (*Wk Monks* 37). In addition to his ministerial responsibilities, Augustine had to spend many afternoons sitting as a deputy for the Roman judicial system. The Roman imperial courts in Augustine's time were so backed up and corrupt that Catholic bishops regularly heard civil cases and were authorized to render judgments. No doubt, while hearing cases, Augustine found himself a firsthand witness to the results of original sin. Human ignorance and weakness were all too evident and operative in the litigation he had to adjudicate.

All these duties made it difficult for Augustine to find the time to retire to and rest in the interior garden of his soul. We all endure the many demands of life, whether they are part of our proper responsibilities or imposed on us by the irresponsibility of others. When we find it difficult to make time and space for prayer amidst the sweat and toil of daily work, we might feel like Adam and Eve, banished from our interior Eden, missing the company of God, unable to walk with the Lord in the garden, in the cool of the evening (Genesis 3:8, 19, 23).

Making time and creating space for interiority requires a concerted effort and a loving discipline, an asceticism that discriminates among the demands of daily life and the needs of others, and at the same time attends to the necessities of the soul. The members of an Augustinian community are called to exercise mutual accountability, to remind and encourage each other to remain faithful to contemplation, and to help each other find the proper balance between prayer and work.

> No one should spend so much time in contemplation that they ignore the needs of a neighbor, nor be so absorbed in action that they feel no need for contemplation of God. What should draw us to contemplation is not escape or laziness, but the opportunity to search for and discover truth, knowing that as we make progress in this search, we share our discoveries with others. (*CG* XIX.19)

***Illumination.*** We already have reflected on how difficult it can be to listen carefully with empathy, even when the other person seeking our attention is someone we love and care for. As we have suggested, pride can lurk in and among our auditory attempts, insisting that our own agenda come first, demanding to maintain control, keeping us from entering the world of the other, or limiting our freedom to imagine what and how it is they suffer. God's grace opens our ears and unseals our love, so that, once healed of our own pride, we can listen as God has listened to us (Mark 7:31-37).

It can be as difficult to listen to oneself as it is to listen to someone else. Shortly after he returned to Africa from Italy in 388, Augustine wrote a little book called *The Teacher.* It is a dialogue between Augustine and his son Adeodatus, who died during or shortly after the composition. Augustine, the recently retired teacher, discusses with his son how important the interior life is, even and especially for students. It is the teacher's job to help young students discover their capacity for interiority, to train them in the habit of listening to themselves.

Augustine identifies learning as an interior process. The teacher's words should stimulate the student to enter the interior court of inquiry and reflection. Words have value only when they invite students to go within their own minds, where the real learning takes place. "Those who are known as pupils reflect within themselves whether what has been said is true, contemplating, that is, that inner truth according to their capacity. It is then that they learn" (*Tchr* 14.45). Augustine's message was not only for Adeodatus, not only for teachers and students in the classroom. It is a general message about interiority for all of us in the school of life. We need to learn, to be tutored in, to acquire the skill of interiority. It takes time and effort. It is an ascetical training.

This process of interior reflection, of listening to oneself, is also a work of integration. It begins with concentrating on what we have heard, read, or experienced. Then, in the quiet of the inner garden of our soul, we examine possible connections between and among our ideas and experiences, searching for relationships, patterns, and logical links. The dynamic inherent in interiority is the progression from the discrete parts and events of our lives toward an interior sense of the whole (*Tchr* 12.40). Augustine, ever the teacher, models for us in *Confessions* how to understand, evaluate, and integrate the different parts of our life experience, and to discern God's providential care as we sort things out. The stories he shares from his life are invitations for us to go within, to listen quietly to ourselves, to wait in prayerful silence, and to receive intuitions of integration that slowly help us make sense and name the truth of our own experience.

Augustine assures us that we are not alone when we withdraw into the silence of the soul. God is also there, in our inner garden, as God originally was in Eden. Augustine affirms that the Eternal Word who created us also resides within us. As we search for an integrated understanding of our life experience and God's part in it, the Eternal Word within us, whom Augustine calls a "secret oracle" (*Tchr* 14.46), moves mysteriously amidst our prayer, within our restlessness, and among our questions. Our interior search for understanding and integration intersects with the divine.

This is Augustine's teaching of divine illumination. God graces our interiority and favors our interior listening with the "inner light of truth" by which the "inner person is enlightened and made happy" (*Tchr* 12.40). The God who "brought light into being" (*Conf* XIII.8.9) is the same God who shines intelligible light within our souls so that we can see the truth of who we are and why we exist. Interiority is not an exercise in isolation. When we withdraw into our soul in contemplation, we encounter the Creator of light and of intelligibility. "Only in your light will we see light" (*Conf* XIII.16.19; Psalm 36:9). When we seek to interpret our lives and integrate the meaning of events, God's love fills our souls "with intelligible light" so that we can discern the pilgrim path that leads to happiness (*Misc 83* 46.2).

## Memory

Book ten of *Confessions* is a long philosophical-theological meditation on the mystery of memory. In books one to nine, Augustine recounted selected events from his first thirty-two years. He then spends book ten asking about what he had just done. What is memory? He has shared many memories with us, along with the prayers, restlessness, and questions that filled the first three decades of his life. He also remembers how he discovered God's saving providence throughout the ups and downs of his young life. But what is the faculty by which he is able to do this?

So in book ten, Augustine stops to ask many questions about the nature of memory itself. His reflections on memory are pertinent to Augustinian spirituality because the work of spiritual interiority is a work of memory. When we retire to the interior cloister of our soul, we encounter ourselves through our memories. "There I come to meet myself. I recall myself, what I did, when and where I acted in a certain way, and how I felt about so acting. Everything is there which I remember having experienced for myself or believed on the assertion of others. . . . This I do within myself in the immense court of my memory" (*Conf* X.8.14).

Augustine speaks of memory as one of the great works of God's creation. We often admire and describe the beauty of "lofty mountains, and huge breakers of the sea, and crashing waterfalls, and vast stretches of ocean, and the dance of the stars" but we fail to wonder at the mystery of memory, its "vast, infinite recess," its role in making us who are, and its place in our spiritual lives (*Conf* X.8.15).

As a work of interiority, the active task of memory is not only to recall, but to interpret and to integrate. The memories that come to us from our own past experiences come to us "in a scattered and disorderly way" (*Conf* X.11.18). We need to "collect" our thoughts, to "recall" the emotions tied to events, and amidst the vicissitudes of life, to "recognize" the stable truths of being, beauty, truth, and goodness that help us make sense of it all. In the interior cloister of our souls, we sit surrounded by all these gifts of memory. Sorting through them one by one, we arrange them so as to discover hidden patterns of integration and graced moments of integrity that slowly disclose the meaning of events and allow us to interpret the purpose of our life.

We cannot always make sense of it all. The work of interpretation, the interior task of integrating the events of our lives, is often "a land hard to till and of heavy sweat" (*Conf* X.16.25; Genesis 3:17,19). In fact, Augustine presents no ready theory of cognitive integration, no spiritual blueprint for remembering. He says simply, "In the end, who can fathom this matter, who can understand how the mind works?" (*Conf* X.16.24). Our memory is a mystery of the second kind, one that confronts us in the very depths of our being, one which we cannot control or comprehend or explain in any satisfactory way. We must bring it to prayer:

O my God, profound, infinite complexity,
what a great faculty memory is,
how awesome a mystery!
It is the mind, and this is nothing other
than my very self.
What am I, then, O my God?
What is my nature?
(*Conf* X.17.26).

One thing that Augustine does affirm: We meet God in our memory. God dwells there, suffused among the scattered, recollected bits of our lives. We have memories of God. At some point in our lives, we heard of God. Somewhere along the way, we were taught about God. "From that time when I learned about you I have never forgotten you" (*Conf* X.24.35). And, even when we were young, we began to pray. "So it came about that even then in boyhood I began to pray to you, my aid and refuge. By calling upon you I untied the knots of my tongue and begged you, in my little boy way but with no little earnestness, not be let me be beaten at school. You did not hear my prayer" (*Conf* I.9.14). Prayer and pain, all wrapped up in the same memory.

In memory, we also encounter one another. While we seek inner quiet and peace, the voices of those who are or have been part of our lives will gradually drift in over the garden wall. Echoes of what others have said or done, or what we have said or done, eventually find us during contemplation. Even as we strive to listen to ourselves, we hear others as well. Augustine's *Confessions* are filled with the memories and voices of many people, named and unnamed persons who were part of his life. He calls them the "witnesses" to his life (*Conf* X.1.1). Among them are his parents, his son, his companion, his many friends, former Manichean associates, famous Roman rhetoricians, and Milanese priests. Some of their voices break the surface of Augustine's text and reach our ears. Others remain submerged, silent witnesses. But we meet them all to some extent in Augustine's exercise of memory, as he seeks to contemplate the meaning of his life through the integrative lens of God's providence.

***Memory and the Mystery of the Total Christ.*** In order to listen to ourselves, we may at times need to hush the many other voices that emerge in memory. However, we should not silence them completely. The mystery of our communion in Christ is part of the mystery of our memory. Christ unites us in his Body with all those who fill our lives and populate our memory. The contemplative exercise of memory provides an opportunity to reflect on our communion with others in Christ. The quiet of our inner cloister offers a ready opportunity for spiritual communion with the Body of Christ, a place to re-member all those, living and deceased, with whom we remain united in Christ.

We often assure other people that we will pray for them, especially when they have entrusted us with their struggling and suffering. The remembered voices of those whom we love and cherish also move us to hold them in prayer. The sound of their voices lingering in our garden is a call to prayer on their behalf. In other cases, the more strident speech of those who trouble us is also a call to prayer for forgiveness, patience, and understanding.

The Eucharist is *the* celebration of memory to which we bring our personal memories and unite them with the mystery of the Whole Christ. We remember those who have "gone before us marked with the sign of faith" (*Eucharistic Prayer*). We remember those we love and those whom we struggle to forgive, even as we ask to be forgiven. Eucharistic memory is not just reminiscence of past events in Christ's life on earth, nor is it indulgence in nostalgic religiosity. It is a celebration of the efficacious mystery of memory. In Eucharist, our memories are united with the memory of God and become one with the communion of saints and Christ.

Ultimately, the Eucharist reminds us that we move in, through, and beyond our memories into the divine mystery itself. When we "lift up our hearts to the Lord," God accepts not only our hearts but all the memories we carry within our hearts. God then lifts us beyond our memories into divinity:

> What shall I do, then, O my God, my true life? I will pass beyond this faculty of mine called memory. I will pass beyond it and continue resolutely toward you, O lovely Light. What are you saying to me? See, I am climbing through my mind to you who abide high above me. (*Conf* X.17.26)

In his classic work *The Trinity*, especially in books ten and eleven, Augustine continues his profound reflection on memory, subsuming it into his great Trinitarian analogy of memory-will-understanding. The many theological and philosophical distinctions in *The Trinity* cannot be explored here. Suffice it to say that the mystery of memory serves to help us meditate on the mystery of God who never forgets us. "Upon you I call, O God, my mercy, who made me and did not forget me when I forgot you" (*Conf* XIII.1.1).

***Memory, Meaning, and Love.*** The "profound, infinite complexity" that is our memory is an active, creative faculty in which we try to discern and interpret the meanings that emerge from the people, places, and events of our past. What Augustine said in *Teaching Christianity* about interpreting Scripture applies to memory. When we read Scripture, he wrote, we must recognize the many levels and layers of meaning in the sacred text: the community for whom it was written; the intentions of the Divine Author; the intentions of the human author; the many meanings that have emerged out of faithful readings of Scripture by communities of faith around the globe and over the ages.

As with Scripture, so with memory. Our memories present us with multiple levels and layers of meanings: about the original events; about the communities of persons that filled our lives at that time; about our intentions and motivations then and now; about what we have since learned about others and how our lives have affected them. In quiet interiority, we study the remembered texts and contexts of our lives, allowing meanings and motivations to emerge and confront us.

The ultimate rule for the exercise of memory is the same as that which Augustine identified as the ultimate rule for interpreting Scripture. We need "to carefully turn over in our minds and meditate upon what we read until an interpretation be found that leads to love (*Tchg Ch* III.15.23)." We apply that same rule when we exercise memory and interpret our lives. We are not alone in that interior task. In faith, we are confident that Christ, the Inner Teacher, sits with us in the cloister garden of our soul, helping us sort through memories. Together with him, we turn over in our mind and meditate upon what we remember until an interpretation of the events of our lives is found that leads to love, to deeper union with him and with all members of his Body.

At the end of book nine of *Confessions*, Augustine asks his readers, present and future, all those he "serves with his heart and voice and pen," to remember his parents at the altar of the Eucharist:

> Let them remember with loving devotion these two who were my parents in this transitory light, but also were my brethren under you, our Father, within our mother the Catholic Church, and my fellow citizens in the eternal Jerusalem, for which your people sighs with longing throughout its pilgrimage, from its setting out to return. (*Conf* IX.13.37)

In this request to remember the two who brought him to life on this earth, Augustine invites us to the table of Christ, to the

Eucharistic altar, which is the source and summit of memory, interiority, and listening.

## Augustinian Contemplative Nuns

These reflections on listening, interiority, and memory call for mention of our contemplative Augustinian nuns. In addition to the various Augustinian communities of mendicant brothers and sisters, and the various third orders and lay associations, the Augustinian family also includes women who live cloistered lives as Augustinian nuns. Their monasteries around the world witness to the contemplative dimension of Augustinian spirituality. Their monastic vocation as Augustinians involves a twofold listening. "Listening to God, and listening to ourselves, to our own history and our struggles. We ourselves come from a never-ending journey of searching and conversion" (Sister Sara Cozzolongo, OSA, Monastery of San Salvatore, Lecceto).

Moved by the innate desire of every human heart for prayer, and driven by the restlessness and many questions that life poses, these women dwell with Christ, the Incarnate Word, in a small portion of the Church, the monastic community. At some point in their lives, a personal encounter with Christ opened the space for a choice, for a radical change of life, and the decision to enter the monastery. Meeting Christ inspired in them the desire to offer their entire existence to the Love that manifests itself in the depths of the human heart: "God speaks in secret, he speaks to many in their hearts; and great is the sound in the great silence of the heart" (*En Ps* 38, 20).

By the witness of their lives and the example of their prayer, our Augustinian nuns remind us of the centrality of interiority and contemplation in Augustinian spirituality. Their vocation enriches all Augustinians. "But while the Church enjoys her delights in the persons of those who rest so sweetly and humbly, here knocking at the door is he who says: 'What I tell you in the darkness, say in the light . . .' (Matthew 10:27). His voice knocks at the door crying:

'Open to me, my sister, my beloved' (Song of Songs 5:2-3)" (*Hom Gos Jn* 57.4).

In addition to their daily prayer and contemplation, the nuns also receive many visitors. The silence of their monasteries, the attentive listening to God that is at the heart of the contemplative life, prepares them to listen to others. It makes them occasions of grace to the many people, young and old, who come to them, seeking understanding, inner healing, forgiveness, and strength. "Contemplation of the face of God—which is personal but never solitary—has two outcomes: communion with our sisters in the monastery, and openness and sharing through listening and witness with anyone who reaches out to us" (Sister Sara). They offer to others what the Lord has given them, for the Augustinian life of contemplation is a life of sharing the superabundant grace of God (*Sol* 1.12.21; 13.22). Like Augustine's early monasteries, their monasteries are places of both contemplation and of service, of availability to those who seek their counsel.

The nuns listen so effectively and efficaciously to others because their lives are organized around listening to God in the depths of their souls. Like John at the Last Supper, Augustinian contemplative nuns lay their heads, so to speak, not only on the heart of Christ, but also on the hearts of those who come to them. The nuns recognize the heart of Christ beating in the breasts of those who wish to pray with them, those who share their restlessness with them, those who bring their questions to them, those who arrive at their doors, like Augustine, "carrying a tattered, bleeding soul that did not want me to carry it" (*Conf* IV.7.12). They receive these visitors with love.

Our contemplative sisters are sacraments of listening, occasions of grace to all who come to their monasteries to pray, to seek peace, to ask for divine illumination. The beautiful cloister gardens at the center of their monasteries remind us to visit the interior cloisters of our souls. "Love for such beauty can have this standard: not only do I not envy it in others, but I also ensure that many desire it with me, strive for it with me, possess it with me, and enjoy it with me. And they will be all the more my friends the more they possess the beloved in common" (*Sol* 1.13.22).

## Chapter Five

# Friendship, Hospitality, and Forgiveness

In *Confessions,* Augustine tells us that friends were an important part of his life. He mentions them frequently: Nebridius, Romanianus, Verecundus, and his closest, longest friend Alypius, the "brother of my heart" (*Conf* IX.4.7). Friends appear during his youth and young adulthood, during his five years in Italy, and upon his return to Africa. Some of his friends became part of the communities in Thagaste and then in Hippo after Augustine became priest and bishop there.

For Augustine, friendship was the foundation of community life. It was also the basis for hospitality to others beyond the community, for extending the values of community into the wider world. And both friendship and hospitality depend on forgiveness to progress and develop as expressions of mutual love and respect.

## The Blessing of Friendship

As a bishop, Augustine corresponded with Saint Jerome, the great biblical scholar. Once, after a testy exchange of letters, Augustine wrote to Jerome referencing their disagreement and suggesting how important friends were amidst the challenges and struggles of life:

> I by no means think
> that you could have become angry
> unless I either said
> what I ought not to have

or did not say it as I ought to have,
for I am not surprised
that we know each other less well
than we are known by our closest
and most intimate friends.
I admit that I find it easy
to abandon my whole self
to the love of them,
especially when I am wearied
by the scandals of the world,
and I find rest in that love
without any worry.
I, of course, feel that God
is in that person
to whom I abandon myself
with security and in whom
I find rest in security.
And in that security
I do not at all fear that uncertainty
of tomorrow stemming from
human fragility. (*L* 73.10)

Augustine was not particularly close to Jerome. They never met in person. In this letter, Augustine seems to suggest that Jerome would better understand his good intentions if, in fact, they were friends. The letter also seems to hint that after reading Jerome's fiery letters, Augustine needed the consolation of friends!

Friendship is a universal human blessing. In book nineteen of Augustine's long work *City of God*, amidst his reflections on life's challenges and difficulties, he wrote these words: "What greater consolation do we have in this human society . . . than the unfeigned faith and mutual love of true and good friends?" (*CG* XIX.8). In the letter he wrote to Proba, whose flight from the sack of Rome had separated her from many friends, he acknowledged her loss. "Without a friend, nothing in the world seems friendly" (*L* 130.2.4). He also consoled her at this particularly difficult time in her life:

> If poverty pinches, if grief saddens, if bodily pain disturbs, if exile discourages, if any other disaster torments, provided that there are present good human beings who know how to rejoice with those in joy, but also to weep with those who weep (Romans 12:15) and can speak and converse in a helpful way, those rough spots are smoothed, the heavy burdens are lightened, and adversity is overcome. (*L* 130.2.4)

Early in *Confessions*, while sorting out his motives for stealing those pears from the neighbor's orchard, he provides a summary statement about friendship, in which he affirms the positive value of having friends and how friendships lead to community. "The friendship which draws human beings together in a tender bond is sweet to us because out of many minds it forges a unity" (*Conf* II.5.10). The words *because out of many minds it forges a unity* recall the beginning of his *Rule*: *live together harmoniously and be of one mind and heart intent upon God* (*Rule* I.3). Augustine saw friendship as the basis of community and as a principle for understanding community.

***Friendship and Community.*** It would be unrealistic to think that Augustine expected all members of a community to "be friends" with each other. To begin with, friend is not a univocal word with only one, specific, explicit meaning. Upon reflection, each of us could differentiate among the many kinds of friendship we enjoy. The dynamics between friends depend on how long they have known each other, what parts of their lives intersect, what values and interests they share in common, their relative personal strengths and weaknesses, what hopes and dreams they may mutually embrace, and so forth. In addition, friendship plays different roles in different societies, and among the different families and social groups within those societies.

Augustine understood friendship as forging and shaping the unity among the members of a community. In his earlier writings, Augustine employed definitions of friendship from classical philosophers such as Plato, Aristotle, and Cicero. Borrowing from them, he describes friendship as "agreement on all things human and divine, along with good will and affection" (*Arg Skps* 3.6.13; *L* 258.1). However, to understand how Augustine used friendship as a way of understanding Christian community, we need to take a closer look at how he came to value friendship not only as an important kind of human relationship, but also as a dimension of the spiritual life.

***Friendship and the Holy Spirit.*** Book thirteen of *Confessions* is an imaginative and symbolic meditation on the first chapter of Genesis. Augustine approaches the Hebrew poem of creation in light of his Christian belief in the Trinity, that is, of God as Father, Son, and Spirit. He interprets the text of Genesis 1:1-2, where it reads "God created the heavens and the earth," as obviously referring to God the Father. He then goes on to read the very first words of Genesis, "In the beginning," as referring to the Son, the Eternal Word, in whom all things have their beginning. Lastly, he finds the Holy Spirit in the phrase "while a wind from God [or the Spirit of God, in Hebrew *Ruach Elohim*] swept over the waters." "And there was your Spirit poised above the waters! Here, then, is the Trinity who is my God: Father, Son and Holy Spirit, creator of the whole created universe" (*Conf* XIII.5.6).

Immediately after this Trinitarian interpretation of the first words of Genesis, Augustine continues to meditate on the role of the Holy Spirit. The image of the Spirit of God hovering over the waters reminds us, he writes, that the same Spirit of God "hovers" over us. He quotes Saint Paul: "The love of God has been poured out into our hearts through the Holy Spirit who has been given us" (Romans 5:5). He enlarges the poetic vision of God's Spirit hovering over the primordial waters by placing us into the vivid imagery of the Genesis text. He asks, with some exuberance, "To whom should I speak, and how express myself, about the passion that drags us headlong into the deep, and the charity that uplifts us through your Spirit who hovered over the waters?" (*Conf* XIII.7.8). Alluding to Baptism, he describes us as swept along and submerged by the floodtide of our restless cares, then to be carried upward by the Spirit of God "in a love for peace beyond all care, that our hearts may be lifted up to you, to where your Spirit is poised above the waters" (*Conf* XIII.7.8).

In this biblical meditation, Augustine traces our sanctification, our immersion into the life of the Trinity, all the way back to the primordial movement of God's Spirit in the act of creation. Participation in the life of God was the original divine intention for us. In his book *The Trinity,* Augustine reaffirms the creative role of the Holy Spirit in our sanctification and identifies divine love for us as the means by which we come to divine life:

> So the love that is from God and is God is distinctively the Holy Spirit; through him the charity of God is poured out in our hearts, and through it the whole triad dwells in us. . . . The Holy Spirit is the Gift of God. And this Gift, surely, is distinctively to be understood as being the charity that brings us through to God. (*Trin* XV.5.32)

In commenting on the First Letter of John, Augustine again identifies divine love as our origin and destiny. "Have you begun to love? God has begun to dwell in you. Love God who has begun to dwell in you, so that by dwelling in you more perfectly, God may make you perfect" (*Hom 1 Jn* 8.12).

As a particular kind of love, friendship is a gift of the Holy Spirit. What Augustine writes about love and the Holy Spirit applies especially to friendship. It is a gift from God that should "be understood as being the charity that brings us through to God." Friendship emerges from the divine community of love that is the Trinity, graces our lives with the love of friends, and pulls us together with our friends into the eternal communion of God. That is why Augustine could write to Jerome that he found it easy "to abandon my whole self to the love of them" and that he could "rest in that love without any worry" and "feel that God is in that person to whom I abandon myself" (*L* 73.10).

***The Holy Spirit as Source of Our Unity.*** Augustinian spirituality affirms that when we love, we have begun to live the very life of God. The gift that is the Holy Spirit is no more and no less than love, love which binds us more closely to each other and to God. When we love, we live and move and have our being in God. Peter Lombard, a medieval commentator on Augustine's spirituality, put it this way: The Spirit of God is the act of love. In Augustine's own words: "If someone is full of love, what is he or she full of but God" (*Trin* VIII.5.12).

Friendship, as a particularly precious kind of love, can be considered the basis of community life in the sense that the mutual love of friends reveals the richness and fullness of divine love that dwells in community. Genuine friendship is a powerful, revelatory example of the power of God that "binds fast together people who cleave to you through the charity poured abroad in our hearts by the Holy Spirit who is given to us" (*Conf* IV.4.7).

Taking friendship at a basic humanistic level, as "agreement on all things human and divine, along with good will and affection," we must conclude that not everyone in an Augustinian community can be a friend all the time, in every way, to every other member of the community. We do not "agree on all things" all the time, be they human or divine. In addition, we may not always be able to sustain our goodwill and affection, given the weakness of our will, the susceptibilities of our affection, and our random inability to understand each other.

But on the level of the spiritual life, everyone in our Augustinian community is a potential friend, because the same Spirit has filled all of us with divine love. The same Spirit moves over the hidden depths of our souls, calling us to divine life and love. The same Spirit lifts us all upward and out of our narrow desires with the healing power of universal love. The following words of Augustine to Proba can inspire every Augustinian community, religious and lay, and encourage every member of every community to strive toward unity in the Spirit:

> Friendship should not be bounded by narrow limits, for it embraces all to whom we owe affection and love, though it is inclined more eagerly toward some and more hesitantly toward others. It, however, extends even to enemies, for whom we are also commanded to pray. Thus, there is no one in the human race to whom we do not owe love, even if not out of mutual love, at least on account of our sharing in a common nature (*L* 130.6.13).

## Hospitality

Saint Possidius was a friend of Augustine who lived with him in the monastery at Hippo. He later became a bishop himself. Possidius wrote a short biography of Augustine not long after his death. In his *Life of Saint Augustine,* Possidius paints a picture of Augustine welcoming guests to his community in Hippo:

> His meals were frugal and economical, at times, however, in addition to herbs and vegetables they included meat for the sake of guests and sick brethren. Moreover, they always included wine. . . . He practiced hospitality at all times. Even at table he found more delight in reading and conversation than in eating or drinking. (*Life* XXII.2.6)

The Augustinian practice of hospitality, like the Augustinian understanding of friendship, is based on the gift of love that is the Holy Spirit. The abiding potential of friendship with other members of an Augustinian community also extends beyond the community. It opens onto the world. You may remember that Augustine did not invite others to withdraw with him to desert places, like the monks in Egypt. He established communities in the midst of towns and cities. These communities were not only houses of contemplation and prayer. They were also centers of service to the People of God, who were their neighbors and potential friends.

In their formation as contemplatives, Augustinian nuns emphasize the connection between their life of intense prayer and their gift of attentive listening. While they live the contemplative dimension of Augustinian spirituality in a more enclosed environment, they still understand their monastic communities to be a spiritual resource for others in the Church and in the world, for those who need the wisdom and insight that is the fruit of their contemplation. Their communities should be

> listening to the reality of the Church, of society, of the world of others, in a cordial openness to broader horizons, without indulging in reassuring answers that are good for everyone. (*Ratio Formationis* of the Italian Augustinian Monasteries 4.3.2 no.144)

Even amidst the solitude and silence of an enclosed contemplative life, they understand their cloister to be a "womb of friendship" with God and with "every brother and sister in humanity" (4.3.2, no.143). Such hospitality was part of Augustine's original vision of community. The last sentence in the *Rule* expresses Augustine's hope that the "sweet odor of Christ" will "spread abroad" and inspire others.

> The Lord grant that you may observe all these precepts in a spirit of charity, as lovers of spiritual beauty, and may spread abroad the sweet odor of Christ by a good life, not as slaves living under the law but as men and women living in freedom under grace. (*Rule* VIII.48)

Augustinian religious communities, then, whether the houses of the friars or the monasteries of contemplative nuns, are centers of hospitality that welcome those who visit. In their own way, Augustinian lay communities also welcome and embrace those who approach, express interest, or occasionally participate in the prayer and activities of the group. All visitors are welcome because "every human being is neighbor to every other human being" (*S* 299D.2)

***Augustinian Community as the Inn of the Good Samaritan.*** In commenting on the parable of the Good Samaritan in the Gospel of Luke (10:25-37), Augustine interprets the inn to symbolize the Church. In Jesus' parable, a priest and a Levite ignore a victim whom robbers beat and left by the side of the road. A Good Samaritan stops and attends to the man. The Samaritan then lifts the wounded man onto his donkey, takes him to a local inn, cares for him, and the next day asks the innkeeper to look after him, promising to reimburse any expenses. The inn, Augustine writes, "is the Church where travelers are refreshed from the journey as they return to the eternal fatherland" (*Ques Gosp* II.19).

The Church, the community of faith, should be where people are welcomed, where they find care and healing. This applies also to Augustinian communities. In his symbolic interpretation of the various elements in Jesus' parable, Augustine highlights phrases like "the consolation of good hope," "the reconciliation of peace," a "fervent spirit," and "the two commandments of love." These are all dimensions of hospitality offered to pilgrims whose journey has led them into the embrace of an Augustinian community.

The parable of the Good Samaritan was Jesus' response to a legal expert who had asked him, "Who is my neighbor?" After telling the parable, Jesus asked the expert, "Which of these three, do you think, was a neighbor to the man who fell into the hands of the robbers?" (Luke 10:36). Augustine elaborates what Jesus' question implies: "He wished to impress on us that every human being is neighbor to every other human being" (*S* 299D.2). Augustinian communities, both religious and lay, living in communion with Christ and one another, should be places where "every human being" is welcome. They should offer safe haven to pilgrims, whether wounded or whole, so they can find, if only for a time, consolation, good hope, reconciliation, peace, fervent spirit, and love of God and neighbor. Writing in another book about the Good Samaritan, Augustine stresses universal hospitality to all. He wrote that we are neighbors of all persons, whether Christian or not: "We ought, therefore, to consider any person a neighbor and not a stranger who we are concerned should not remain a foreigner" (*Ag Lying Con* 6.15).

***Friendship and Hospitality as Mutual Support.*** Some monks, either in Hippo or Thagaste, wrote to Augustine for clarity about Saint Paul's words in *Galatians* to "bear one another's burdens, and thus you will fulfill the law of Christ" (Galatians 6:2). In his response, Augustine points to friendship as an important way of fulfilling the law of Christ to love our neighbor. He may have had in mind friendships within the monastery. But his response also applies to hospitality, that is, to relationships with people beyond the community in the wider population. His response can be read as a meditation on friendship and hospitality, and the need for discernment in exercising them.

He begins by suggesting an image taken from the Roman historian Pliny, who wrote about how a herd of stags support one another when crossing a river together. These animals inspire us to "bear one another's burdens."

> When they cross over a body of water to an island in order to feed, they arrange themselves so as to put the burden of their heads, which are heavy with antlers, upon each other in such a way that the one behind stretches his neck and places his head on the one before him. And since there has to be one who leads the rest and has no one in front of him to lay his head on, they are said to take turns, so that the one who is in the lead and is worn out by the burden of his head goes to the end of the line, and the one whose head he bore when he himself was first, takes his place. Bearing one another's burdens in this fashion, they cross over the water until they come to solid ground. . . . Nothing so proves a friend as bearing a friend's burden. (*Misc* 83 LXX.1)

Augustine suggests that we are all part of the herd of humanity. We are to help each other along the journey of life. We are to help shoulder burdens carried by the members of our immediate community. We are also called to lighten the loads and ease the yokes of those in the wider society. We are to offer friendship to each other and to all those trying to stay afloat and reach a place where they find nourishment for their souls.

***Discernment in Friendship and Hospitality.*** In his message to the monks, Augustine goes on to reflect on discerning the dynamics of friendship and on the prudence required when offering hospitality. Augustine gives advice about complementary weaknesses and strengths in relationships. There will be times when our strength will help us carry the burden of a friend who is weak. At other times, when our strength ebbs or when we realize that we are not constitutionally fit to handle a challenge, we should not hesitate to reach out to a friend who can help relieve us of the deadweight crushing us. We need to listen to ourselves in order to discern our condition and assess our strengths and weaknesses. Such attentiveness to oneself and to one's friends helps relationships grow to mutual benefit. There are also differences of personality. One person might be a talkative extrovert, another a quiet introvert; one caught in grief, another given to anger. Such differences of personality, character, and situation must be considered in negotiating friendship. Such differences and susceptibilities also must be weighed when offering hospitality.

Augustine also reflects on how often when we first meet someone, we are impressed by their good traits and unaware of their negative ones. How do we manage the relationship when negative qualities begin to emerge? Or, our first meeting with someone may leave a bad impression. Yet, over time, we see more and more of their good, positive qualities. He urges tolerance, patience, and understanding over time, so that mutual understanding can grow and rash judgments avoided, lest we miss an opportunity for true friendship. There is also the situation when we meet someone who remains shy and reserved around us because they perceive us as socially or intellectually superior. He encourages us to reach out with courtesy and humility and invite such hesitant persons to move beyond status to authentic personal encounter.

In this long response to the monks' question about bearing one another's burden, Augustine shows that he is not naïve about the complexity of friendships nor about the prudence required for judicious hospitality. In the end, however, he coaxes us to both:

> The friendship of no one who seeks to become our friend should be rejected—not that he should be received at once, but that we should be open to receiving him and to treating him in such a way that he can be received. For we can say that a person has been received into our friendship when we dare to disclose all our thoughts to him. (*Misc* 83 VXXI.6)

## Forgiveness

All of us have had an experience of friendship troubled or broken, trust betrayed or exploited, hospitality abused or refused. Augustine was too much of a realist to expect that spiritual ideals of friendship and hospitality were exempt from human frailty. We can paraphrase his comment in the *Rule* about pride destroying good works and suggest that pride lurks even in good friendships, seeking to destroy them. So, he says, we need to be vigilant. "But we count peace as no more than an uncertain good, for we do not know the hearts of those with whom we wish to be at peace, and, even if we could know their hearts today, we still would not know what they might be like tomorrow" (*CG* XIX.5).

Religious communities do not assure protection against difficulties in relationships. In the monastery, he wrote, he had met the best and worst of men. "Just as I have come with difficulty to know any better persons than those who have made progress in monasteries, so I have not come to know worse people than those who have fallen in monasteries" (*L* 78.9). This was in a letter he wrote to the monks, clergy, and lay people in Hippo about the public dispute between a monk and a priest, who were accusing each other of some kind of sexual sin. We will return to this letter shortly, for it shows how Augustine approached disputes and accusations within community.

Even when our friendships are honest and authentic, they can cause us pain. We fret over our loved ones. In book nineteen of *City of God*, Augustine lists the many concerns we have for our friends. We worry about their health. We worry about their safety—kidnapping was a practice all too common in Augustine's day. Even worse, we worry they might lose their freedom—kidnapped victims were often sold as slaves and transported to some distant country. So while our friendships bring us consolation, joy, and peace, they can also cause us concern, sorrow, and strife. It is important, Augustine advises, to reflect on our responsibilities in friendship and the motivations behind our behavior toward friends.

***Taking Responsibility and Understanding Motivation.*** Augustine confesses personal responsibility for difficulties in his own friendships over the years. In recalling the incident of the theft of pears, he reflects back on the nature of the relationships he had with his adolescent friends. "What an exceedingly unfriendly form of friendship that was" (Conf II.9.17). With the perspective of age informed by faith, he critiques the "gang-mentality" and "camaraderie with my fellow-thieves" that bound them together. Their association lacked any substance of true love. It was inflamed only "by the stimulation of conspiracy" (Conf II.8.16). While it seems a harsh criticism to level at adolescent boys, Augustine recounts the event as an example of seeking and searching for the motivation behind relationships. What is it, exactly, that we think we share in common as friends? What binds us together? Why are we friends?

Augustine is just as critical of his seventeen-year-old self, newly arrived to study in the exciting metropolis of Carthage, "where the din of scandalous love-affairs raged cauldron-like around me" (*Conf* III.1.1). He indulged in what the city had to offer. "Loving and being loved were sweet to me, the more so if I could also enjoy a lover's body; so I polluted the stream of friendship with my filthy desires and clouded its purity with hellish lusts" (*Conf* III.1.1). His experience taught him that "friends with benefits" is friendship prone to problems. Such liaisons lead to "the iron rods and burning scourges of jealousy and suspicion, of fear, anger and quarrels" (*Conf* III.1.1). Again, it is a question of motivation in relationships.

In book four of *Confessions,* Augustine moves from the confusion and volatility of adolescent relationships to a more clear-sighted vision of the pride that compromised his friendship with someone he had known since childhood in Thagaste. They had played together as children, and renewed their relationship once Augustine returned from his studies in Carthage. Augustine convinced this friend to become a Manichean, as Augustine himself had done during his years in Carthage. Augustine wrote, "I did love him very tenderly . . . and similarity of outlook lent warmth to our relationship" (*Conf* IV.6.7). But their relationship "fell short of true friendship, because friendship is genuine only when you bind fast together people who cleave to you through the charity poured abroad in our hearts by the Holy Spirit who is given to us" (*Conf* IV.6.7). The relationship on his side, Augustine admits, was based not on the charity of the Spirit but on his need to control and manipulate his friend.

Augustine describes how his friend fell ill with fever, probably malaria. During the illness, the young man's family had him baptized while he was unconscious. Upon learning this, Augustine strongly disapproved and told his friend so when he regained consciousness. But the young man rebuffed Augustine, and "with amazing, new-found independence warned me that if I wished to be his friend I had better stop saying such things to him" (*Conf* IV.4.8). This left Augustine "aghast and troubled." He decided to wait until his friend was back to normal health, and then "I would be able to do what I liked with him" (*Conf* IV.4.8). This is an astonishing confession of bold narcissism on Augustine's part, a far more pernicious motive than the mischief or lust behind his adolescent behaviors.

The fever soon returned, and his friend died in Augustine's absence. "And I was not there," Augustine writes with self-accusatory abruptness (*Conf* IV.48). The death of his friend sent Augustine into black grief and prolonged depression. In one of the most moving descriptions of grief in Latin literature, Augustine replays the agony his life had become without his friend. His grief was complicated by his own fear of dying, as well as with the sense that life was not worth living without his friend. He indicts God: "You took him from this life after barely a year's friendship, a friendship sweeter to me than any sweetness I had known in all my life" (*Conf* IV.4.7). Augustine finally had to leave his hometown. It held too many memories of their friendship. So, along with his companion and their little son, he returned to Carthage.

There, in a city that had witnessed his adolescent excess, the older and much sobered Augustine finally began to heal and emerge from grief. And, in what can seem a paradoxical resolution, it was friendship that gradually restored him over the passage of time and the changing of seasons. "What restored and re-created me above all was the consolation of other friends" (*Conf* IV.8.13). He then goes on to give a beautiful description of friendship in community:

> Such signs of friendship sprang from the hearts of friends who loved and knew their love returned, signs to be read in smiles, words, glances and a thousand gracious gestures. So were sparks kindled and our minds were fused inseparably, out of many becoming one. (*Conf* IV.8.13)

In his review of these earlier friendships in his life, Augustine invites us to reflect on motivation and discernment as two essential components of forgiveness. When we find ourselves called to forgive another person for what they have done to us or failed to do for us, reflecting on their motivation as well as our own can help move us toward forgiveness. To do that, we need to withdraw into ourselves, to enter the interior garden of our souls, in order to reflect. We need to listen to ourselves, our deeper selves; we need to listen to what our friend has said or failed to say; we need to listen to what God, the origin and source of all friendship, has to say.

Listening involves the work of integration, of slowly making sense of all that has happened in the relationship. Interior listening, reflection, and integration lead to a better understanding of what has happened, what has been said or left unsaid, and what has been done or left undone. We need to discern our part in it as well as our friend's responsibility. Understanding born of interior reflection, inspired by the Spirit's love, can move us slowly toward a forgiveness that is honest about the human ignorance and weakness that afflict all of us, and with a desire to heal the rift if at all possible.

Forgiveness may sometimes involve the fraternal correction that Augustine speaks about in chapter four of the *Monastic Rule*. It may call for direct confrontation when we have suffered injury. In *Sermon* 82, Augustine preached on Matthew 18, where Jesus tells us to forgive one another not seven times, but seventy-seven times. In this sermon, Augustine says that forgiveness may require calling out the offender, which, however difficult, is an act of love challenging the person to repentance. It is part of the responsibility of forgiveness. In another sermon, he preached on the First Letter of John. Augustine elaborates on how we should go about forgiveness, how to discern the decisions necessary to forgive and move along. However you do it, he says, do it with love:

> Once for all, then, a brief precept is given to you: Love, and do what you want. If you are silent, be silent with love; if you cry out, cry out with love; if you chastise, chastise with love; if you spare, spare with love. The root of love must be within; nothing but good can come forth from this root. (*Hom* 1 Jn 7.8)

***The Order of Love.*** What spirituality brings to friendship is what Augustine called the order of love. He affirms the beauty of all creation, including the beauty of friendship and community. They are part of God's creation. "Were these beautiful things not from you, none of them would be at all" (*Conf* IV.10.15). But if we love them instead of or apart from God, if we assign them the permanency of the Eternal, if we love them as if they will never cease to be, we are confusing creature for Creator. Only God is infinite, eternal, everlasting. Augustine says the very nature of our love is to seek a beloved that will never end, never go extinct, never depart, because "you have made us for yourself, O Lord." When we put such subliminal expectations upon our friendships, we are bound to be disappointed.

The solution is to love all the beautiful things of creation *in God*. "If sensuous beauty delights you, praise God for the beauty of corporeal things, and channel the love you feel for them onto their Maker, lest the things that please you lead you to displease him" (*Conf* IV.12.18). He applies the same principle to the love of friends, families, and communities. "If kinship with other souls appeals to you, let them be loved in God, because they too are changeable and gain stability only when fixed in him; otherwise they would go their way and be lost. Let them be loved in him" (*Conf* IV.12.18). It is not a matter of loving others less because we love God more. It is a matter of loving friends because our faith affirms the divine presence within the fabric of our love. "Let us love him, for he made these things and he is not far off, for he did not make them and then go away: they are from him but also in him" (*Conf* IV.12.18).

Pride disorders love. When, like Adam and Eve, we presume omniscience in our relationships, when we itch for control or lust for dominance, then we undermine our friendships and disrupt our communities. When, like Christ, we humble ourselves and seek to love others for their own sake rather than our own, when we love them as fellow creatures of a loving God, then we will experience a peace that is the tranquility of ordered love. "The peace of all things is the tranquility of order, and order is the arrangement of things equal and unequal that assigns each its due place" (*CG* XIX). For relationships among friends, within families, and in communities to be peaceful, we need a humility that acknowledges God as Creator, the Word as present throughout all creation, and the Spirit as pouring out divine love into our hearts. Our friendships, our families, our communities are all gifts *from* God, gifts *of* God. The love we find there is the love "that brings us through to God" (*Trin* XV.5.32). When we remember that, we will live together in the tranquility of order and peace.

***Do Not Let Your Love Grow Cold.*** In the open letter he sent to the entire Catholic community in Hippo about the dispute between a monk and a priest in that city, Augustine models both humility and forgiveness. A priest who lived in the monastery in Hippo, Boniface by name, accused one of the monks of a sexual sin—we don't know exactly what. The monk's name, ironically, was Spes, which means hope in Latin. Spes, in turn, accused his accuser of the same charge. The whole matter became public, and so Augustine decided to address the scandal openly.

Augustine wrote that no one should be surprised that such scandals happen, even among religious persons. Jesus himself warned that scandals will come: "Woe to the world because of scandals" (Matthew 18:7). He expressed his sorrow over what had happened, and understood the sorrow it had caused among the whole Church in Hippo (*L* 78.1). The case troubled Augustine for a long time, since he had no way to prove who was lying. He did not know who to believe, though he wrote, "I was more inclined to believe the priest" (*L* 78.3). He sent both of them off to a shrine for a retreat that would hopefully bring the truth to light through an honest confession.

In the meantime, Augustine addressed the upset and turmoil in the community. He made several points that can help us deal with times of trouble and distress in our friendships or our communities. While everyone was saddened by what had happened, he said, "Do not let your love grow cold" (*L* 78.2). As bishop, he would have to adjudicate the case, following the rules established by the Church for such problems. But do not, he pleaded, give in to gossip, detraction, and false suspicion. Such things would only make the problem worse. And do not assume a "holier than thou" attitude. He then humbly asked, "Pray, of course, for me for fear that I may perhaps be found to be rejected after preaching to others, but when you boast, boast not in me, but in the Lord. For however vigilant may be the discipline of my monastery, I am human, and I live among human beings" (*L* 78.8).

When scandal, accusation, or revenge, or any other problem infects one of our friendships or invades our community, Augustine would give us the same advice he gave his people long ago amidst a very trying time in their life together. To the sentiments and hopes he shared in his letter to the people, we can add some words from a homily he preached around the same time, words of encouragement for all those who strive to love and forgive one another:

> Ask God that you may love one another. You should love all people, even your enemies, not because they are your brother or sister, but so that they may become your brother or sister, so that you may always be aflame with such love. (*Hom 1 Jn* 10.7)

# Chapter Six

## Humility, Poverty, Peace

Around the year 410, Augustine received a letter from a Greek student by the name of Dioscorus. He had been studying in Africa and was about to return home. Before he left, however, he wanted Augustine's opinion on some fine points of Cicero's philosophy, in case scholars back home in Greece quizzed him on the topic. He did not want to be judged "unlearned and stupid."

Augustine wrote a long letter in response. He never gives the lad the information he requested. Rather, Augustine advised him not to worry about being embarrassed. "So what" if they quiz him and he doesn't know the answer? Though Augustine himself quotes many philosophers in the letter, he reminds Dioscorus that true philosophy, the love of wisdom, is not achieved through academic performance, nor through the "vanity of human praise." Only humility leads to truth. In this letter, Augustine makes his well-known statement about the way to truth. "The first way is humility; the second way is humility, and the third way is humility, and as often as you ask, I would say this" (*L* 118.3.22). There are other commandments, Augustine continues, but "unless humility precedes and accompanies and follows upon all our good actions, . . . pride tears the whole benefit from our hands" (*L* 118.3.22). Augustine tells Dioscorus that knowledge afforded by philosophy is valuable. But without faith in Christ, the seeker of wisdom will never reach truth. "Our Lord Jesus Christ humbled himself in order to teach us this most salutary humility" (*L* 118.4.23).

## Humility

We have seen how the Incarnation is central to Augustinian spirituality, and that at the center of the Incarnation is the mystery that God "emptied and humbled himself" in the person of Jesus (Philippians 2:7-8). The mystery of the humility of God is the inspiration for Augustinian spirituality, the exemplar for the spiritual life, the paradigm for the search for truth. The question presents itself. What does a spiritual life based on humility look like?

Humility is a recurrent theme in the history of Christian spirituality. Unfortunately, it has sometimes been interpreted as humiliation, as self-abasement. The humble Christian, some people have advised, is the one who denies their gifts or devalues their accomplishments. Of course, an all too common side effect of this kind of energetic self-effacement is pride in having achieved it. Pride in one's humility can "tear the whole benefit from our hands." In effect, such counterfeit humility seeks praise, looking for others to admire them "as though they themselves were their own good" (*CG* 12.1). Augustine admits that years after his conversion and well into his ministry, he still "hankers for praise," and "garners every little tribute of approval . . . to bolster some fancied pre-eminence." "This is a real temptation to me, and even when I am accusing myself of it, the very fact that I am accusing myself tempts me to further self-esteem" (*Conf* X.38.63). Note his incessant quest to unearth motivation!

However, contrary to false humility and self-abasement, the second great commandment "You shall love your neighbor as yourself" (Mark 12:31) presupposes a healthy love of oneself, even pride in oneself. Augustine did not have a problem with all self-love. We should accept, rejoice, and thank God for who we are and what we can do. At the end of book one of *Confessions*, after reflecting on his youth, Augustine prays a prayer of thanks for his talents and his very existence:

> In a living creature such as this
> everything is wonderful and worthy of praise,
> but all these things are gifts from my God.

I did not endow myself with them,
but they are good,
and together they make me what I am.
He who made me is good, and he is my good too;
rejoicing, I thank him for all those good gifts
which made me what I was, even as a boy . . .
and what you have given me
will grow and reach perfection,
and I will be with you;
because this too is your gift to me—that I exist.
In a living creature such as this
everything is wonderful and worthy of praise,
but all these things are gifts from my God.
I did not endow myself with them,
but they are good,
and together they make me what I am.
He who made me is good, and he is my good too;
rejoicing, I thank him for all those good gifts
which made me what I was, even as a boy . . .
and what you have given me
will grow and reach perfection,
and I will be with you;
because this too is your gift to me—that I exist.
(*Confessions* I.20.31)

How do we achieve this balance between rejoicing in our gifts and talents, and acknowledging God as their source? How to take credit and give credit at the same time and in the proper order? As always, Augustine tells us to look to Christ, the mystery of the humility of God, and the "demonstration of how much value God put on us and how much he loved us" (*Trin* 13.13). Our faith in the mystery of the Incarnation needs to become part of our daily spiritual lives, so that we can "progress in his strength," so that the "power of charity be brought to perfection in the weakness of humility" (*Trin* 4.2). We need God's grace to rescue us from the kind of self-love that is self-promoting, self-indulgent, self-absorbed;

the kind of self-love that bears a secret contempt for God as well as for neighbor (*CG* XIV.13). How to receive this grace?

***Praying the Psalms.*** Even before his Baptism, during his long retreat at a villa in Cassiciacum, in Northern Italy, Augustine began praying the psalms. He finds in the psalms "a remedy, an antidote" for pride: "How loudly I began to cry out to you in those psalms, how I was inflamed by them with love for you and fired to recite them to the whole world, were I able, as a remedy against human pride" (*Conf* IX.4.8). The words of the psalms became "the intimate expression of my mind, as I conversed with myself and addressed myself in your presence . . . words of my own, interspersed with yours" (*Conf* IX.4.8). It is in prayer, specifically in prayer inspired and informed by the psalms, that Augustine finds the repeated administration of healing grace that finds and uproots the "appetite for perverse exaltation . . . to become and to be one's own principle" (*CG* XIV.13).

The love he had for the psalms as a new convert continued throughout his life and ministry. In the early years of his ministry, Augustine composed meditations on the first thirty-two psalms. He would go on to write and preach running commentaries on all one hundred fifty psalms, a unique accomplishment in early Christian literature. Years later, as he lay dying in Hippo, which was under siege by Vandal tribes, he asked that the words of the psalms be printed in large letters and hung on the walls of his room to accompany and console his final hours. Augustine loved, prayed, and preached the psalms because the psalms were an encounter with Christ. The mystery of the Eternal Word is present in the words of the psalms, as in all of Scripture. But in the psalms, a Christian meets and engages in a unique way with the human Christ. The psalms, which express the gamut of human emotions, are a living expression of and testimony to the humanity of Christ. When we pray the psalms, we pray and feel and reflect with Jesus of Nazareth at our side and in our hearts.

The authors of the New Testament interpreted Old Testament passages as prophetic of the Messiah. The Gospels are filled with references to Hebrew Scriptures, which they see fulfilled in Jesus. John refers to Jesus as the new Moses (John 1:17). Paul calls Jesus the new Adam (Romans 5:12-21; 1 Corinthians 15:22). In the Gospel of Matthew, Jesus prays the words of Psalm 21:2 from the cross and makes them his own: "My God, My God, why have you forsaken me?" (Matthew 27:46). This way of reading the Old Testament, as fulfilled in the New, continued into the early centuries of Christianity. Augustine received this tradition and expressed the relationship between the two testaments this way: "The New is hidden in the Old and the Old is revealed in the New" (*Ques Hep* II.73; *Ex Ps* 105.36).

However, Augustine intensifies this relationship between the two testaments. He finds in the Hebrew psalms not only prophetic image and hopeful longing for the Messiah, but the real presence of Christ. When you read or hear a psalm, you encounter the healing person and saving presence of Jesus. This may seem surprising, at first, because the psalms express the vast array of human feelings and passions. Augustine was exceptionally sensitive to the psalmist's capacity for human sentiment and constantly refers to the variety of emotions found in the psalms. The psalms enthusiastically shout joy and thanksgiving and quietly echo peace and contentment. However, they also vent resentment and anger; they stew with jealousy and envy; they tremble with fear and anxiety; they stare into chasms of despair; they vow revenge. They even dare to challenge and accuse God of forgetting Israel and the covenant. How can such disquieting prayer and troubling complaints be associated with Jesus? But that is Augustine's point. When the Word became flesh, he took on all that is human, but sin. To express anger, jealousy, envy, fear, anxiety, and even to peer into the depths of despair is not sin. It is human. Even to confront God is human. "My God, my God, why have you forsaken me?" (Psalm 22:1).

In the psalms, we meet the human Jesus, the Word *made flesh*. When we meditate upon a psalm and seek to understand its meaning, our voices, our feelings, our doubts, and fears, as well as our praise and thanks, are united with the voice and feelings and prayer of Christ. When we pray the psalms, the Word of God takes flesh in us. The psalms, Augustine claims, are the voice of the *Totus Christus*, the Whole Christ. In the words of the psalms, Christ speaks his own sentiments. At the same time, we members of Christ's Body give voice to our hopes and prayers. When praying the psalms, both we and Christ find in the sacred text words to express the whole spectrum of human experience. When we pray the psalms with Christ, we become Christ. "The Head was crying out on behalf of the members, and the Head was transfiguring the members into himself" (*Ex Ps* 30[2nd].3).

Even when the psalms ask forgiveness for sin, Christ's love for us is so strong that he joins his voice with ours. How can some words of the psalms that speak of guilt and sin be attributed to Christ? Because Christ's love for us makes us one with him. So, even though the words refer to us and our sin, Christ makes them his own. "Do you not understand that it is charity that makes us one in Christ? Charity cries out to Christ from our hearts, and charity cries out from Christ on our behalf. . . . If then he is the head and we are the members, one single individual is speaking. . . . The one Christ speaks" (*Ex Ps* 140.3).

The psalms, therefore, bring us deeper into the mystery of the Whole Christ. They are the real presence of Christ, in a way analogous to the Eucharist. When praying the psalms, we are in communion with Christ and with each other. We are "organically" part of Christ. "This is how we should hear Christ speaking. Yet each one of us should at the same time hear his or her own voice, since we are all organically parts of Christ's body" (*Ex Ps* 140.3). Augustine finds the sacrificial love of God that we celebrate in the Eucharist to be present in the psalms as well:

> The body of Christ, the unity of Christ, is crying out in its anguish, its weariness, its affliction, in the distress of its ordeal. It is one single person, a unity grounded in an individual body, and in the distress of its soul it cries from the bounds of the earth: "from the ends of the earth I have called to you, as my soul grew faint (Psalm 60:3[61:2])." (*Ex Ps* 54.17)

As when celebrating the Eucharist, so when praying the psalms, we are united with Christ in his death and resurrection. "Harken to a single voice here. . . . We too were there [at Christ's death]. He took over into himself our lowly body and transformed it, configuring it to his own glorious body (Philippians 3:21). Our old self was nailed to the cross with him" (*Ex Ps* 142.9). When praying the psalms, we join the mystery of "the Son's humble acceptance of humanity, the sacrament whereby the Word was made flesh" (*Ex Ps* 71.3). We are transformed, transfigured, when we pray the psalms. We might even appropriate the word transubstantiated to name this mystery.

The psalms, then, are the "remedy" and "antidote" to pride. Our engagement with the psalms provides the opportunity for continuous conversion by association with the humble Christ. They are daily spiritual exercises for the soul that effect our gradual sanctification not by our own merits, but by the power of the Spirit who unites us with Jesus. Praying the psalms in communion with Christ "prepares our will" through an ever-growing realization that Christ loves us unconditionally (*Ans Jul* VI.10.11). God's love, experienced and effected through the psalms, heals our pride, teaches us authentic humility, and conforms us to the image of the Son (Romans 8:29).

Saint Ignatius invited his followers, when reading the Gospel stories, to imagine themselves as one of the characters in the story, or as a bystander witnessing an event, such as a miracle or healing. Augustine issues a similar call regarding the psalms. But it is not to exercise the imagination. It is to enter mystery. It is a call to profess faith in the mystery of the Whole Christ by joining our voice with his and letting him take our words to make them his own. It is an affirmation that these ancient Hebrew prayers bring us and Christ into ever deeper communion. The psalms both reveal and effect the mystery of the Whole Christ.

Augustine called the psalms "the school of Christ" and invited his congregation to become "scholars in the school of Christ" (*Ex Ps* 79.1). This calls to mind Augustine's idea of co-inhabitation, by which he describes what happens when students and teachers listen to each other. He writes that when teachers and students listen carefully to each other, they "live within each other" (*Instr*

*Bg* 12.17). They dwell within each other's mind and heart. Listening is an act of love that strengthens the bond between persons.

We can apply his idea of co-inhabitation to the mutual indwelling between all members of the Body of Christ that the psalms reveal and effect. When we pray the psalms together "in the school of Christ," Christ the Teacher not only listens to us. His love for us is a desire or movement to become one with us (*Misc 83* XXXV.1). When God listens to us as we pray the psalms, Christ makes our words his own. He dwells in us. He "inhabits" us, becomes one with us, and pulls us ever deeper into the mystery of divine love.

## Poverty

Augustine understood poverty in light of humility. The two are "so closely related that no one can be called a 'poor man of God' as was Augustine, without being humble" (*Constitutions of the Order of Saint Augustine* II.32). With regard to the spiritual life, the question is not how much or how little of this world's resources a person has. We are all God's poor, Augustine reminded his congregation: "However much you may have, you are God's beggar" (*S* 123.5). After all, we repeatedly come before God and together pray the words that Jesus taught us all, begging God to "Give us this day our daily bread" (Matthew 6:11).

Augustine did not see wealth as a reward for leading a good life, nor poverty as punishment for sin. He was a realist who understood how human beings treated each other. The unjust distribution of wealth across society is not a matter of divine providence, but the result of all sorts of evil machinations by those who control resources and redistribute them (*S* 18.1–4). Whatever our fiscal state or status, God is present with us and will use our varied circumstances to call us to conversion of heart, to humility (*Ex Ps* 66.3; *S* 18.1).

Augustine often preached and commented on the text of the Gospel that had moved Antony of Egypt to sell his possessions, give to the poor, and follow Christ (Matthew 19:16-28). As the Gospel story goes, the rich young man who had approached Christ went away sad because he could not do what Christ had asked. He had great wealth. This led Jesus to observe, "Truly I tell you, it is hard for someone who is rich to enter the kingdom of heaven. Again I tell you, it is easier for a camel to go through the eye of a needle than for someone who is rich to enter the kingdom of God" (Matthew 19:23-24). How to appropriate these words of Jesus for the spiritual life? How is poverty part of Augustinian spirituality?

***Augustine to His People.*** Augustine often had two audiences in his congregation, two categories of the faithful who would hear this Gospel passage, and for whom he had to interpret it. The majority audience were the lay people of his diocese: farmers, fishermen, and sailors; merchants who had businesses and those who worked for the Roman administration; soldiers and visitors who were traders from other lands; women who had responsibility for homes and families. Some of these were people of limited means; most were very poor. Still others, a very few, were wealthy landowners, on whose estates many of the others worked.

In addition to this great variety of lay Christians, there was often a second category in the congregation. These were members of the monasteries, the men and women who had followed Jesus' call to give what they possessed to the poor and follow him. They would join the congregation for Mass.

In similar fashion, the Augustinian family today includes the vowed religious men and women who have heard the words of Jesus to the rich young man and have responded by giving up all personal possessions, attending to the poor, and following Jesus. In addition, there are the thousands of lay people who are affiliates of the Order, or members of the many lay associations and third orders. These lay Augustinians, like Augustine's congregation in Hippo, come from all walks of life. They represent all economic levels of society, from poor to rich, on all five continents. Augustine's message to his congregation so many years ago still rings true for the Augustinian family today. For poverty, like humility, is an important dimension of Augustinian spirituality.

Augustinian poverty is a matter of attitude toward the things we have and use. It concerns how we relate to the resources at our disposal, however extensive or limited they may be. As always, the Augustinian question is one of motivation. What is behind how we approach and manage what we have? How do we feel about what we possess? What moves us to behave as we do when using, sharing, or hoarding our "things." As is the case with humility regarding our personal gifts and talents, Augustinian poverty seeks a balance between joyful gratitude for our material blessings and grateful acknowledgment of God as their source.

After all, Augustine reminds us, whatever we have, however much we own, we have received it all. Everything comes from God. Ultimately, nothing is of our own making. In one sermon, Augustine imagines God speaking directly to his congregation: "What, after all, did you bring with you when you came here? Everything I have created, you found here when you were created; you didn't bring anything, you won't take anything away from here . . . you were all born naked" (*S* 123.5).

***To the Rich.*** The rich should not boast about their wealth. "The primary worm in the apple of riches is pride. It is an evil grub that gnaws the whole away, and reduces it all to ashes. So, 'command them not to have proud thoughts, nor set their hopes on the uncertainty of riches'" (*S* 85.3; 1 Timothy 6:17-19). Rich people who boast of their wealth, who set their hopes on it, who put it at the center of their identity, practice a self-justification based on their possessions or accomplishments. Instead of gratitude for what they have received from the Creator, their boasting is an exercise in self-love, a daily drill in self-congratulation. It is a self-promoting and self-indulgent kind of pride that bears a secret contempt for God and sometimes a not so secret contempt for neighbor, especially poor neighbors (*CG* XIV.13).

Augustine's message to the wealthy is to "Pull up greed, plant love, I mean, as greed is the root of all evils, so love is the root of all good things" (S 72.4). Your wealth is a good thing, he tells them, if it is used to produce good. "You want to have gold and silver; yes, here, too, I say, it's something good, but only if you use it well . . . if it is put to good use" (S 72.4). He continues with advice that still rings true for upwardly mobile people who want also to live a spiritual life:

> You want to get a promotion; that is a good thing, but here, too, only if you use it well. How many people are there for whom promotion has been the occasion of their ruin? And how many people are there for whom promotion has been a means for doing good. (*S* 72.4)

But it is not only a matter of charity for the less fortunate, of doling out money or food or property. The rich must grow in awareness of the systemic injustice around them. All persons, rich or poor, are equal in the eyes of God. "A Christian should never set himself up over other human beings. . . . If you wish to be better than another person, you will grudge to see that person as your equal. Therefore, you ought to wish all equal to yourself" (*Hom 1 Jn* 8.8).

In contrast to the equality of all persons made in the image of God, there is the unequal distribution of goods across societies and around the globe. Augustine challenges the rich in his congregation "to grow increasingly generous in giving away whatever we have to spare. If we hold onto only what we need, we shall find that there are many superfluous things in our possession" (*Ex Ps* 147.12). He enlists them in addressing the inequities in society: "God does not demand much of you. He asks back what he gave you, and from him you take what is enough for you. The superfluities of the rich are the necessities of the poor. When you possess superfluities, you possess what belongs to others" (*Ex Ps* 147.12). Even more directly:

> Do you think it is a small matter that you are eating someone else's food? Listen to the apostle; we brought nothing into this world, yet a full table is set before you. The earth and its fullness belong to God. God bestows the world on the poor; God bestows it on the rich. (*S* 29.2–4)

Again, he presses them to look at the motivation behind their generosity, urging them to move beyond charity to justice:

> For we mustn't wish that there be unfortunates, so that we may be able to exercise the works of mercy. You give bread to the hungry, but it would be better if no one were hungry and you gave to no one. You clothe the naked. Would that all were clothed and there weren't this need. . . . (*Hom 1 Jn* 8.5)

The goal for those fortunate enough to be wealthy and influential is to create a society that, as far as possible, eliminates poverty and injustice; to work for a society where the truth of our equality before God is reflected in our equality before each other. Augustine tells them, "Choose to be equal, so that both of you may be under the one to whom nothing can be offered" (*Hom 1 Jn* 8.5).

In his commentary on Genesis, in book thirteen of *Confessions*, Augustine traces God's demand for social justice all the way back to the story of creation. When describing the emergence of the seas, of sweet waters and dry land with its multitude of grasses, plants, and trees, Augustine discerns in the text a meditation on mercy and justice. Just as God's Word brings forth the abundant variety of living things, God also commands that "the soil of our souls grow fertile in works of mercy" and that "we fructify in love of our neighbors by assisting them in their bodily needs" (*Conf* XIII.17.21). We should "take care of the needy in the way we would wish to be relieved were we in the same distress" (*Conf* XIII.17.21).

But it is not just a matter of giving to the poor, not just "the easy provision" of grain or grass that is harvested relatively easily and stored for distribution. What God calls for is that we become like sturdy trees. That we:

> supply the stout, oak-like protection of a fruit-bearing tree, which in its benign strength can lift an injured person clear of the grasp of a powerful oppressor, and furnish protective shade by

> the unshakable firmness of just judgment. (*Conf* XIII.17.21)

It is not just a matter of mercy. True charity calls for justice, for concerted efforts to oppose and deconstruct systems that perpetuate injustice and allow the wealthy to exercise their lust for domination. It is a matter of justice, of "the unshakable firmness of just judgment."

***To the Poor.*** Neither should the poor boast about their poverty, be it the voluntary poverty of religious life, or the impoverished circumstances caused by economic forces and systems. Members of monasteries who have given up their possessions to follow Christ in religious life should not take credit for their sacrifice. They should not "consider that their laudable way of life should be credited to themselves, rather than to the grace of God" (*Ex Ps* 71.3). Their pride can make them "think their virtue is of their own making, and boast as though they had not received it" (*Ex Ps* 71.3).

Augustine has a similar message for the economically poor members among the laity in his congregation. He tells them:

> You that are poor, listen to Christ. . . . Most of you are poor; you at least must try to understand. . . . Any of you inclined to boast about your poverty, beware of pride, or you may be beaten to the post by the rich who are humble. . . . Don't boast about your poverty, if they ought not to boast about their riches. (*S* 85.2)

He warns about the paradox of poverty. "You sometimes find a poor person who is proud and a rich one who is humble" (*Ex Ps* 131.26). He pushes the idea further. Even those who are poor and oppressed by the wealthy, even those subjugated by social injustice, can unfortunately be proud in the sense of being self-righteous: "From this you can discern what he would have been like if he had been an owner of property" (*Ex Ps* 131.26). By contrast, "You come across another person who has an ample household, lush lands, many estates, and plenty of gold and silver, yet he knows that these are not to be relied upon. He humbles himself before God and uses his wealth to do good" (*Ex Ps* 131.26). A humble, generous landowner versus a proud, resentful self-owner.

The problem in both cases, whether it is the self-congratulatory pride of the rich or the cupidity of the poor, is avarice. The problematic motivation is greed, the rapacious desire to own, possess, and control however much or however little you have, and always to want more. "God," Augustine says, "is not concerned about our resources but about our greed. He judges a person on the cupidity that drives him to lust for temporal things, not on the resources he has not managed to get his hands on" (*Ex Ps* 131.26).

Christ astonishes and discourages the disciples when he tells them, "It is easier for a camel to go through the eye of a needle than for someone who is rich to enter the kingdom of God" (Matthew 19:24). But then he looks at them, the Gospel says, and reassures them. "For mortals it is impossible, but for God all things are possible" (Matthew 19:26). Commenting on this passage, Augustine reassures his listeners that all who ask, be they rich or poor, "will be given the strength to turn from temporal desires to a charity that is eternal, and from pride to humility" (*Ques Gosp* 2.47). Avarice, like pride, is rooted in the will, in a will that chooses created things, however good they are in themselves, over the Creator. Avarice and pride are complicit in the displacement of the Creator. Pride sidelines the Creator and centers the self. Avarice supplants the Creator with things. More often than not, the displacement is a mix of self and things. Both avarice and pride are part of our "appetite for perverse exaltation . . . to become and to be one's own principle" (*CG* XIV.13).

Augustine has already recommended the "remedy" and "antidote" for avarice. It is the same as that for pride. Prayer, especially prayer with the psalms, calls us, rich and poor, to continuous conversion in union with the humble Christ. They are the daily spiritual exercises we all need for our gradual sanctification by the power of the Spirit who unites us with Jesus. Praying the psalms in communion with Christ "prepares our will." It uproots the avarice that infects our souls by proclaiming Christ's unconditional love for us, whether we are rich or poor (*Ans Jul* VI.10.11). God's love experienced through the psalms heals the illness of avarice, prevents the contagion of pride, and fortifies us to work for the justice that honors our equality before God.

## Peace

In book nineteen of *City of God*, Augustine describes the nature of peace. "Peace is the tranquility of order" (*CG* XIX.13). Our body is at peace when all of its parts are working together in an orderly balance to keep us healthy. Our heart is at peace when our desires are under control. Our mind is at peace when we act authentically, according to our convictions. Our soul is at peace when we humbly honor God as our Creator and redeemer. A home is at peace when authority and obedience are honored by members of the family. Societies are at peace when members live according to ordered agreement, without aggression and avarice. "The peace of the whole universe is the tranquility of order. And order is the arrangement of like and unlike things in their proper place" (*CG* XIX.13).

We can and should strive for such peace. However, Augustine realizes that in this life there will never be perfect peace. Equality and justice are ideals toward which we strive and for which we pray. But we are still on the way, still on pilgrimage, still trekking through disorder. We are still "students in the school of Christ," needing to learn true humility, to practice evangelical poverty, to accept the transformative grace given us by the Word Made Flesh through Scripture and sacrament. In this world, our peace is always threatened by "fierce resistance from vexations, craving, wants and weariness" (*Ex Ps* 84.10).

Worldly peace is compromised by the disorder that results from pride and avarice at all levels: Disorder in our families when pride poisons relationships; disorder in our cities when avarice diverts resources to those who already have them; disorder in our nations and around our planet when both pride and avarice infect the souls of leaders who use power to fill their pockets and secure their positions. Nonetheless, Augustine urges, in such a world we can and should work for whatever peace we can achieve, a peace that "defends and seeks an accommodation among human wills with regard to the things that pertain to humanity's moral nature" (*CG* XIX.17). In such a world, Augustinian spirituality can be a voice, an influence, a "pilgrim society" of people from "all languages" with "differences in the manners, laws, institutions . . . and nations" from which they come, working together for the dignity of all of persons whom they know God loves equally.

Perfect peace awaits us only in the end. In the Kingdom of God, pride will be vanquished forever and God will be at the center, "the object of our contemplation." There, avarice will finally have ended, and only "God will be our common possession." There, God will be in place of whatever gifts we have received in this life and "God will be our peace, perfect and total" (*Ex Ps* 84.10). "A peace made pure will reign among God's children: they will all love themselves as they see themselves full of God, and God will be all in all" (*Ex* Ps 84.10).

# Part Three

## Mission

To speak of mission is to ask what Augustinian spirituality offers the Church and the wider world. The Augustinian principles of interiority and communion can deepen the experience of faith for Catholics and Christians of all denominations. Augustinian spirituality also offers hope to all people of goodwill with its vision of humanity transformed by the universal truth of divine love, and with a willingness to engage in loving conversation.

In that sense, Augustinian spirituality has a responsibility to share the wisdom of its tradition and the practice of its principles with those who inquire and accept an invitation to "come and see" (John 1:38).

God will be the end of our desires: who will be seen without end,
loved without satiation, and praised without weariness.
And this gift, this feeling, this activity,
like eternal life itself, will be shared by all.
*City of God* XXII.30.1

Ipse finis erit desideriorum nostrorum, qui sine fine videbitur,
sine fastidio amabitur, sine fatigatione laudabitur.
Hoc munus, hic affectus, hic actus profecto
erit omnibus, sicut ipsa vita aeterna, communis.

## Chapter Seven

# Hope

Addressing an October 2024 meeting of those gathered in Rome for the Synod on Synodality, Pope Francis called hope "the humblest of virtues." Compared to the profession of faith and the exercise of charity, hope might indeed seem humble. It stands there, quiet and unassuming, wedged in between faith and love, glancing out toward us on occasion. However modest it might appear, it is hope that pulls us through when faith is tested and love becomes difficult. Hope may be humble, but it is hardy.

Pope Benedict reminded us of the importance of hope. We need it, he wrote in his Encyclical *Saved in Hope*, to assure ourselves that the commitment of faith and the sacrifice of love are ultimately worthwhile (*Saved in Hope,* no. 1). We need to trust that our faith and our love are leading somewhere. We need to be confident that there actually is a goal we will reach. When life becomes arduous, when our prayer seems unheeded, our restlessness relentless, our questions unresolved, then it is hope that keeps us believing, hope that maintains our love. Toward the end of *Confessions*, Augustine expresses his own need for hope amidst doubt and difficulty. He confesses that when he hears "the unceasing taunt" of so many people, "Where is your God?" he, too, begins to ask along with the psalmist, "Where are you, my God?" (*Conf* XIII.13.14–14.15):

> I still slip back and become an abyss once more, or rather it feels like that. . . . But my faith takes me to task, that faith which you have kindled, like a

> lamp, on my nocturnal path: "Why so sorrowful, my soul? . . . Trust in the Lord; his word is a lamp for your feet." Keep your hope high and persevere. (*Conf* XIII.13.14–14.15; Psalm 42)

## Hope for the Church

Augustine's original communities of prayer were located in or near the cities and towns of North Africa. As we have noted several times, their common life of interior contemplation was not only for the benefit of the monks and nuns who joined the monastery. Their religious dedication was for the benefit of the whole Church. Augustine hoped that these communities would be a leaven of faith and love in the Christian community at large and "spread abroad the sweet odor of Christ" (*Rule* VIII.48).

When the Order of Saint Augustine was founded in 1244, the Church asked it to follow Augustine's vision of religious life in service to the Church. "Following the example of Saint Augustine, love for the Church brings us to a total availability for its needs, by accepting the tasks which the Church asks of us, according to the charism of the Order" (*Constitutions of the Order of Saint Augustine* II.35). The Constitutions go on to specify that "availability for service to the Church constitutes one of the essential characteristics of Augustinian spirituality." Notice the explicit connection between Augustinian spirituality and Augustinian service. Their connection is inherent and intrinsic because service "is an exterior activity springing from a deep and strong interior community life" (*Constitutions* II.36). In whatever particular kinds of ministry Augustinians find themselves, ultimately it is their spirituality that is their gift.

Augustinian spirituality has a special relevance to the needs of the Church today because so many Catholics, indeed so many Christians of all denominations, are seeking the kind of interiority and community that Augustinian spirituality offers. This twofold desire for attention to the interior life and for the experience of authentic community has emerged repeatedly in the discussions and statements of two recent Synods of the Catholic Church.

***Synodal Listening.*** We identified listening as an important component of Augustinian interiority: listening to oneself, listening to Christ the Teacher within one's soul, listening to the members of one's community in order to discern and respond to their particular needs. The wider Church hungers for this wisdom of interior listening and attentive community. The yearning to be heard has been expressed by the Church itself, meeting in Synod, that is, meeting to listen to each other and to discern together the movement of the Holy Spirit within the Church community.

The multi-year Synod on Synodality, convened by Pope Francis in 2021, stresses the importance of listening for the life of the Church. It is a major theme in the documents of the Synod and a guiding principle of the many Synodal meetings and discussions. The final document of the Synod stresses the importance of interior listening for a vibrant spiritual life:

> A synodal spirituality flows from the action of the Holy Spirit and requires listening to the Word of God, contemplation, silence and conversion of heart. A spirituality of synodality also requires asceticism, humility, patience and a willingness to forgive and be forgiven. It welcomes with gratitude and humility the variety of gifts and tasks distributed by the Holy Spirit for the service of the one Lord. It does so without ambition, envy or desire for domination or control, cultivating the same attitude as Christ who "emptied himself, taking the form of a slave." (Philippians 2:7; *Final Document* Part I, no. 43)

This description of the kind of spirituality espoused by the Synod reads like a description of Augustinian spirituality, almost a table of contents for this book. The Synod document makes the

Augustinian connection between community and the spiritual life: "No one can progress along the path of authentic spirituality alone; we need support, including formation and spiritual accompaniment, both as individuals and as a community" (*Final Document* Part I, no. 43). The kind of spirituality the Church hopes for today already exists in and among lay and religious Augustinians, insofar as they strive to live an Augustinian spiritual life harmoniously in a community "intent upon God with one heart and one soul."

Listening as a spiritual exercise was not a new theme initiated at the Synod on Synodality. The previous Synod in 2018 on "Young People, The Faith and Vocational Discernment" also highlighted how important it is for the Church to listen to all its members, especially the youth and young adults who are its future. This Synod was called so that the Church could listen to young people's concerns. Or, to put it in Augustinian terms, the Synod's purpose was to invite young people to pray together, to share their restless hearts in attentive community, and to raise their questions in the hearing of Church leaders. Three hundred young adults participated in this consultative process, traveling to Rome in March 2018. Another fifteen thousand participated online. The in-person and online participants represented many countries and twenty different language groups. Their collaboration resulted in a seven-thousand-word preliminary document.

This document affirms that "lots of young people, having lost trust in institutions, have become disaffiliated with organized religion and would not see themselves as 'religious.' However, young people are open to the spiritual" (*Final Document from the Pre-Synodal Meeting,* no. 5). In their own voice, the young people who worked together to write this document claimed that "religion is no longer seen as the main stream through which a young person searches for meaning. . . ." They also expressed their disagreement about some of the Church's teachings on sexual morality and health care. Some claimed that the Church even increases the distance between them and Jesus (no. 6).

The document goes on to describe the situation among young Catholics. "There are many young people who relate to God solely on a personal level, who are 'spiritual but not religious,' or focused only on a relationship with Jesus Christ . . . and see the Church as irrelevant" (no. 7). Young people, the document proclaims, are looking to the Church for "companions on the journey," for "mentors who seek holiness," for "confidants without judgment, . . . who acknowledge their humanity" (no. 10). Yet so often what they find in the Church are religious leaders who are "disconnected and more focused on administration than community-building" (no. 7).

Such claims can be discouraging for those who work within the Church and care about its mission. However, there is reason for hope. Despite such reservations and disagreements, these young people still want to be part of the Church. That desire was evidenced in their willingness to participate in the Synodal process and in their hope that the Church and its leaders would hear their questions. Furthermore, the bishops who met several months later responded to the issues raised by the youth themselves and acknowledged "the desire for life in love and the healthy restlessness that is found in the hearts of young people" (*Post Synodal Document* no. 59). Several years later, the Synod on Synodality took note of the concerns expressed by youth and young adults. It sought to "assure them thoughtful and patient accompaniment; in particular, the proposal of 'an experience of accompaniment in view of discernment'" (*Final Document of the Synod* no. 62). It refers frequently to a "spirituality of accompaniment," especially for young people (nos. 43, 62).

***Augustinian Spirituality ~ Synodal Spirituality.*** The various dimensions of Augustinian spirituality that we have focused on in this book correspond to the earnest desires expressed by the youth and young adults during their Synod and reaffirmed by the Synod on Synodality. The desire for relationship with Jesus Christ among Catholics and other Christians echoes Augustine's search for God and his discovery of the humility of God in Jesus, the Word Made Flesh. Augustine's affirmation of our unity with Christ and with each other in the Body of Christ speaks to their longing for community that attends to the interior life of the soul and the needs of all its members. Augustinian friars, sisters, and laity can take their experience of spiritual accompaniment in community and share it with other Christians whose experience of Church may have been limited to administrative concerns or even disconnected from their lives altogether.

The interiority and communion of Augustinian spirituality have much to offer the wider Church. In that sense, its "mission" is clear. It is a mission of hope. Augustinian spirituality offers hope not only to the youth and young adult Catholics who want to remain part of the Church and also want to be heard. Older Catholics have endorsed and identified with many of the questions and concerns expressed by younger Catholics. As we have seen, Augustine spent most of the pages in his *Monastic Rule* listing the circumstances and problems among members of the community that should be discerned, identified, and responded to, with prudence and love. He would offer these same counsels from his *Rule* to the Church today. Listen to each other; recognize differences; respond to needs; love and support one another harmoniously, being of one mind and soul intent upon God.

Augustinian spirituality offers hope to those looking for a spiritual life based on faith in Christ, and practiced in communities intent upon God. With its counsels of interiority, contemplation, friendship, hospitality, forgiveness, humility, and poverty, Augustinian spirituality is a sign of hope for the Church striving to live the Gospel in today's world. Pope Leo brings Augustinian spirituality to the Universal Church. In his first address to the Church and the world, he proclaimed, "I am a son of Saint Augustine, an Augustinian, who said: 'with you I am a Christian and for you I am a bishop.' In this sense, we can all walk together towards that homeland that God has prepared for us." Pope Leo's leadership, inspired by his Augustinian spirituality, offers hope to the youth and young adults of the Church, and to all those of any age seeking "a spirituality of accompaniment in view of discernment."

## Hope in Dialogue with Others Beyond the Church

Moving beyond the Church, one can ask what Augustinian spirituality might offer to members of other religions, or to people who do not belong to any religious or spiritual tradition. Based on Christian faith in the Incarnation, death, and resurrection of Jesus, Augustinian spirituality may at first seem irrelevant to those who do not share that faith. But we can focus the question a bit more carefully. We can ask, what do interiority and communion bring to interreligious dialogue? What does an Augustinian spiritual life based on listening, friendship, hospitality, humility, and poverty offer to partners of goodwill who join inter-spiritual conversation?

***Interreligious Dialogue.*** The Vatican's Dicastery for Interreligious Dialogue identifies four forms of interreligious dialogue which can help us reflect on how both religious and lay Augustinians can relate to members of other faith traditions (*Dialogue and Proclamation* nos. 42–46). The first two forms are what the document calls the *dialogue of life* and the *dialogue of action.* The *dialogue of life* simply refers to the many ways in which people strive to live in an open and neighborly spirit, "sharing their daily joys and sorrows, their persistent human problems and preoccupations."

Augustinian religious and lay communities are often neighbors to people from other religious traditions. Many Augustinian communities are located in large cities and so are part of the religious and ethnic diversity around them. As the world grows more interconnected, we all regularly encounter people from other religious and cultural traditions; interreligious contact in daily, local life is inevitable for many of us. In some countries, Augustinian communities may be part of a minority Christian population, living among Muslim, Hindu, Shinto, or Buddhist majorities. In any case, Augustinian friendship and hospitality can inspire outreach to neighbors and citizens across religious difference, remembering Augustine's counsel to Proba, "There is no one in the human race to whom we do not owe love" (*L* 130.13).

The *dialogue of action* refers to how people from various religious backgrounds work together for justice and peace and cooperate for the integral development and liberation of people. This goes beyond neighborly friendship and simple courtesy to intentional collaboration. It involves meeting and working with members of other faith traditions to address the challenges and concerns they face together in the wider civic society. As Augustine reminds us in *City of God*, we can and should work together for whatever justice and peace we can achieve in this life, collaborating with people of "all languages," navigating "differences in manners, laws, institutions . . . and nations" for the mutual benefit of all persons. Augustinian spirituality extends its careful listening and attentive caring beyond the limits of the immediate community and the Church to the wider world. It seeks active dialogue and alliance with others to cooperate for justice and peace, to "defend and seek an accommodation among human wills with regard to the things that pertain to humanity's moral nature" (*CG* XIX.17).

The third form of dialogue, *dialogue of theological exchange*, refers to academic or pastoral programs where people strive to deepen their understanding of various religious traditions and to appreciate each other's spiritual values. There are many priests, brothers, and sisters in the various Augustinian religious orders, as well as many lay Augustinians, for whom this form of dialogue is part of their ministry as theologians and teachers. I have engaged in this type of exchange for many years and found it immensely enriching of my faith as well as of my understanding of Augustinian spirituality. I recall an event that provides an example of this kind of dialogue.

At an interreligious conference at Oxford University a number of years ago, an Indonesian Muslim surprised me by quoting Saint Cyprian's phrase, "No salvation outside the Church." He knew about Cyprian, a third-century bishop of Carthage. He also knew that a century later, Augustine repeated Cyprian's words. Needless to say, he was a bit put off by the phrase. He asked me for an explanation. He wanted to know if I, as a Catholic and a lay Augustinian, believed that he, as a Muslim, could not be saved. Over the years, I have had several dialogue partners who, like him, had a rudimentary knowledge of Augustine. Usually, that meant they knew the Augustine invoked by medieval theologians and ecclesial hierarchs to bolster arguments for the superiority of Christianity over other religions.

I had to sharpen my recollection of the context of this statement. I explained that Augustine was repeating Cyprian's mid-third-century claim of "no salvation outside the Church" (*S Ch Caes* 6). However, Augustine's repetition of Cyprian's phrase must be understood within its context. Augustine was in the midst of the Donatist controversy. He was encouraging Donatists to come back to the Catholic Church, and specifically to stop persecuting, maiming, and killing Catholics, including members of Augustine's own clergy and congregation. He thought that reminding them of the words of Saint Cyprian, a hero-martyr whom the Donatists admired and respected, might get them to stand down and return to the Catholic Church.

My conversation with the Indonesian Muslim led to a good theological exchange about the importance of understanding the original context of a theological statement in order to interpret its meaning. We also discussed Augustine's respect for the grace of God beyond the Church, a topic to which we will return shortly. All in all, this *dialogue of theological exchange* with my Indonesian colleague was a fruitful one—more fruitful than Augustine's frustrating and largely unsuccessful attempts to get the Donatists to listen to reason.

The fourth form is the *dialogue of religious experience*. It relates directly to what Augustinian *spirituality* has to offer those beyond the Church. In this form of dialogue, people share their spiritual lives, their experience of prayer and contemplation, and their seeking for God, the Holy One. It might also be called *inter-spiritual dialogue* because it focuses on the depth dimension of religion. Spirituality reaches through and beyond the external components of religion, that is, beyond doctrine, morality, and ritual, to the interior relationship with God that underlies the visible aspects of religion.

This form of dialogue may involve different types of shared prayer, contemplative practices, and deep conversation about how one's religious or spiritual tradition understands and approaches God. It provides a sacred space of attentive listening to the participants' commitment, questions, and convictions. In such a meeting of mutual trust and shared listening, Augustinians can share their faith in Christ and how it leads to a spirituality of interiority and communion, as well as the practice of a spiritual life based on listening, friendship, hospitality, humility, and poverty. Such encounters are precious experiences, filled with moments of divine grace and spiritual healing. The Trappist monk, Thomas Merton, was an advocate and leader for this kind of inter-spiritual dialogue.

Some who participate in inter-spiritual dialogue experience what is called "holy envy." This is the discovery of a teaching or practice in another religion that may not exist in one's own, or at least not to the extent that it does in the other tradition. That discovery leads to a gentle "envy" of what the other tradition offers its adherents and may encourage exploration of how one might appropriately incorporate some aspects into one's own spiritual life. I have found, for example, that dialogue partners from other religions often marvel at the Christian teaching of the Incarnation and the radical immanence of and communion with God to which it invites Christians.

I, in turn, have found elements in other religions to enrich my own practice and appreciation of faith. For example, sitting with one of my Muslim students as he read and prayed the mellifluous Arabic of the Holy Qur'an led me to a deeper appreciation of Islamic respect for the sacred text. I witnessed the text's ability to sanctify him as he drew his breath, allowed the language to shape his mouth and bend his body, trusting all the while that it was also shaping his mind and heart. It led me to examine my respect for the Bible and how I might show it greater reverence in daily practice. Another example of holy envy was that of a dear colleague of many years at Merrimack College. He was a philosopher of religion and an expert in Buddhism. He and his wife, both Catholics, had integrated Buddhist meditative practices into their daily recitation of the Divine Office over decades of faithful prayer and practice.

***Jewish-Christian Dialogue.*** One singular instance of interreligious dialogue is Jewish-Christian dialogue, vital for all four forms of *life*, *action*, *theology,* and *spirituality.* In the dialogue of religious experience, Christians should stand in awe of all that the Hebrew tradition and Jewish faith have given us. From the sacred texts of the Hebrew Bible, including the psalms, to forms of worship borrowed from the ancient liturgies of temple and synagogue, to Jewish understandings of God's unity and transcendence, to prayer as sacrifice, thanksgiving, and praise, Christians are deeply in debt to the religious and spiritual traditions of Judaism.

We have looked at how Augustine read and interpreted the Hebrew psalms, and how they led him ever deeper into the mystery of Christ. Augustine acknowledged the debt Christians owed to Jews. Certainly, he argued and debated with the Jews in his region and lamented their rejection of Christ as Messiah. Nonetheless, he respected the divine providence at work in their history and their destiny. He opposed persecution of the Jews of his day and the violence against Jews championed by other Fathers of the Church. Jewish scholar Paula Fredricksen argues convincingly that Augustine's theological and ecclesial influence protected Judaism from the threat of annihilation at the hands of other Christian leaders and communities.

Today, we can appreciate and share Augustine's interpretation of the psalms and the rest of the Hebrew Bible in light of our faith in Christ. But we can do so without also assuming that Christians have superseded or replaced the Jews as God's Chosen People. It is a matter of gratitude for what we as Christians have received from the Jews, honoring their tradition with respect, and expressing contrition for the persecution of Jews wrought by many Christians over many centuries.

***Spiritual But Not Religious.*** Today, there is also a growing interest in spirituality among many who do not practice or belong to a particular religion. Such people emphasize an individual quest for meaning and purpose. They may borrow teachings and practices from different religions, including Christianity, but their quest does not necessarily involve commitment to any one religious tradition or adherence to its teachings. However, they evidence the sincere desire of a restless heart, struggling to find the inherent meaning and ultimate purpose of our human existence. Some appeal to a personal God and understand the spiritual life to involve a quest for relationship with God. Others, by contrast, may assume only an impersonal cosmic force that permeates the universe, before which one stands in ambiguity and uncertainty. Still others remain agnostic about a transcendent being or power of any type, personal or impersonal.

Amid the religious diversity and spiritual pluralism that characterize our contemporary world, Augustinian spirituality takes its place as a religious spirituality, a Christian spirituality. It brings its faith and its values to the world in the hope that it might enrich those beyond the Church with its wisdom and insights into the human condition, and also learn from them. It can apply the four forms of dialogue recommended by the Dicastery for Interreligious Dialogue when reaching out to those affiliated with other faiths, or to those who are spiritual but not religious. These are all ways to offer Augustinian friendship and hospitality, and to discover together how we can support and encourage one another as spiritual pilgrims. We turn now directly to Augustine to see what he had to say about other religions and how his thoughts on this question might enrich our contemporary participation in interreligious and inter-spiritual encounters.

***Letter 102.*** Sometime between 406 and 412, Augustine responded to a request from a priest in Carthage, Deogratias by name. Deogratias had asked Augustine to respond to several questions raised by an unnamed pagan in Carthage. This pagan inquirer was himself a dear friend of Augustine, who was keen to have the man become a Christian. One of the questions raised by this friend, an issue apparently much discussed in the cosmopolitan city of Carthage, concerned the salvation of non-Christians. If Christ is the one and only way to salvation, as Christians claimed, what about all people in the history of humanity who never knew Christ? The question had a corollary: If Christianity is a universal religion, why did God choose a particular time and place to reveal the Gospel, and so, to that extent, limit access to the truth?

One hears the same or similar questions today, as I did from my Indonesian colleague. Such questions come both from those who profess other religions and from many who identify as spiritual but not religious. If, as some Christians believe, explicit faith in Christ is necessary for salvation, what about the great majority of human beings throughout history, and prehistory, who never even heard of Jesus? What about the billions of people on earth today who never get the chance for a reliable hearing of the Gospel? Has chance and happenstance doomed them, even though they are good people leading moral lives of love and respect for others? In past centuries, the Catholic Church responded to such questions with the teaching called the "Baptism of Desire." This states that if all these people *had* heard the Good News about Jesus, they *would have* believed and requested Baptism. Such desire is good enough for salvation, it reasons. Whatever the value of such teaching, Augustine's response in *Letter* 102 is much more vigorous. It reflects both his Christian commitment as well as his awareness of difference, and it enriches dialogue.

In this letter, Augustine affirms his Christian belief in the Eternal Word of God, who was present "in the beginning" and through whom all things were made. He reprises his meditations on Genesis. It is a matter of faith, for Augustine, that the Eternal Word of God pervades all creation and history. All things were created and are sustained through the Word. "In him there is the wisdom and knowledge for directing and governing all creation with respect to what should be done about it and when and where" (*L* 102.11). Augustine then expounds on this doctrine in light of his friend's questions about particularity. Even before God spoke to Abraham and chose the Hebrews as his people, Augustine asserts, the Eternal Word of God, present in all creation and all history, was available to all people. Before the beginning of salvation history as recounted in the Bible, God offered salvation

> to all those from the beginning of the human race who believed in him and understood him somehow or other, and lived pious and just lives according

> to these commandments [a reference to the Ten Commandments], whenever and wherever they lived; [such persons] were undoubtedly saved through him. (*L* 102.12)

Though they had "different ceremonies and sacraments, . . . other names and signs than now, . . ." Augustine continued, they *shared the same faith* and received *the same salvation* as Christians, from the One God and God's Eternal Word. Underneath and within the great variety of religious practices of the human race, Augustine affirms the presence of divine grace operative for the salvation of those who accepted God's offer. Years later, when reviewing his writings, Augustine stressed this idea that all just persons throughout human history are saved by the same divine grace that saves us, not by any merits of their own (*Revisions* 31.58). Divine grace was present and active in their customary sacraments, their native religion, and their household piety. The Word of God, who would become flesh in Christ, was somehow present and active, though hidden, in human history from the beginning. The 1991 document from the Dicastery for Interreligious Dialogue, *Dialogue and Proclamation*, which we have already referenced, reflects Augustine's understanding of the efficacy of other religious belief and practice (*Dialogue and Proclamation,* nos. 16–21).

Augustine emphasized the responsibility of Christians to practice their faith and celebrate their sacraments, which are the revealed and divinely appointed channels and occasions of grace. However, while they live with the assurance of divine revelation in Christ and the testimony of the Scriptures, Christians must not preclude the salvation of others. They must allow that divine providence arranges "what is fitting and proper for any time," and that God approaches human beings in different ways. Divine providence "surpasses human intelligence and is derived from the same source from which providence itself cares for things" (*L* 102.13). Augustine refers to the mystery of this universal offer of salvation as part of divine wisdom "in which there perhaps lies hidden far more deeply another divine plan" (*L* 102.14).

This letter expresses Augustine's conviction that the Word of God was present and active, offering salvation to those who responded in faith, who "understood him somehow or other," and who lived good lives, no matter when and where they lived. Augustine bases his confidence in this universal offer of salvation not in "human intelligence," but in God's plan for humanity, "hidden far more deeply," buried in the recesses of divine providence. He employs the same theology of mystery in *Letter* 102 that he uses when writing about Christian sacraments, that is, the mystery hidden in words and symbols. The different ceremonies and sacraments, names and signs provided various ways that the Divine Word approached these scattered children of Adam and Eve and allowed them to respond to God in prayer and sacrifice (*L* 102.16–21). Clearly, Augustine does not limit a spiritual life, empowered and enriched by divine grace, to baptized, practicing members of the Church.

It is instructive to remember that letters in Late Roman Antiquity were considered public documents and were often read in small conversation groups as well as in wider community circles. Augustine would have been aware of the public notice his letter would receive. It is a call to us contemporary Augustinians to listen with deep spiritual sensitivity to our brothers and sisters from other traditions for how they have heard and received the mystery of divine love within their own religious contexts and spiritual traditions.

However, there is a proviso. Augustine's mission, both as a Christian and as a bishop, was to preach the Gospel. The revelation of God in Christ changed everything for him and, he believed, also for all humanity. Despite his expansive view of the universality of the Word of God, Augustine still desired that his pagan friend become a Christian, "before it was too late." He writes that his friend can continue to ask as many questions as he wants after Baptism (*L* 102.38)—a permission the ever-inquisitive Augustine would have to grant anyone.

We can infer from the text of *Letter* 102 that Augustine might allow that God's Word was universally available not only in pre-Christian history, but also to his contemporaries in and beyond the Roman Empire who had not yet had the Gospel preached to them. Nonetheless, he assumed that this state of affairs was being remedied by the missionary work of the Church across the world. He believed that the Gospel would soon be available to everyone. Rejection of the Gospel after hearing the Word, in his view, does not allow for any default to the kind of universal salvific activity of God available before or apart from salvation history.

He knows that hypocritical Christians can cause scandal and thereby alienate present and potential believers from the same Church that brings them the Gospel. He addresses in many places the question of sinfulness among members within the Church and saintliness beyond the Church. Just as there are members of the Church who are "wolves," so there are "sheep" in the wide world beyond the borders of the Church (*CG* I.35, XIV.1 and XIX.17; *Hom Gos Jn* 45.12). Nonetheless, his sense of mission focuses his attention on spreading the Good News about Jesus Christ. He is convinced that ancient human longing for the divine and the prophecies of the Old Testament all have been fulfilled in Christ. Thus, he professes his faith in the Word Incarnate, even amidst his affirmation of the universality of salvation through the Eternal Word.

This is a tension familiar to many Christians engaged in interreligious dialogue or in conversation with spiritual but not religious persons in our own day. It is the tension between Christian conviction and commitment, and a concomitant desire to follow Augustine's counsel for the interior life: to listen. We cannot afford today to limit within narrow bounds the spiritual exercise of listening. It is not only an essential component of Augustinian community. It is also vital for the Order and for whole Church to remain "open to the world, . . . and feel ourselves in solidarity with the human family and involved with its concerns" (*Constitutions* II.35). The mission of Order as well as the Church is to listen to those beyond the Church, "to focus its attention on the world, the whole human family along with the sum of those realities in the midst of which it lives; . . . created and sustained by its Maker's love, fallen indeed into the bondage of sin, yet emancipated now by Christ" (*Gaudium et Spes—Joy and Hope,* no. 2).

The universality of Augustine's spirituality embraces the "anxious questions about the current trend of the world, about the place and role of humans in the universe, about the meaning of its individual and collective strivings, and about the ultimate destiny of reality and of humanity" (*Gaudium et Spes—Joy and Hope,* no. 2). The mission of Augustinian spirituality is twofold. It is to be prophetic about its foundation in the mystery of Christ as the fullness of the revelation of divine love, and so confess its surrender to the sacrificial love of Christ. At the same time, it seeks "solidarity with, as well as respect and love for the entire human family with which it is bound up" and desires to "engage with it in conversation about these various problems" (*Gaudium et Spes—Joy and Hope,* no. 3). It is a twofold commitment: commitment in faith to Christ and to one another in the Body of Christ; and, commitment in love to all members of the human race. It is that twofold commitment that can be a source of hope and encouragement in dialogue across difference.

If we could return for a moment to Augustine's language about the Whole Christ. His elaboration of Saint Paul's teaching of the Body of Christ has a universalism about it. His assertions in *Letter* 102 about the ubiquity of divine grace in human history and its multiple religious and spiritual expressions reflect several passages about the mystery of the Whole Christ. One example, which we have already cited in chapter two, is worth repeating here:

> All of us together are the members of Christ and his body; not only those of us who are in this place, but throughout the whole world; and not only those of us who are alive at this time, but what shall I say? From Abel the just right up to the end of the world, as long as people beget and are begotten, any of the just who make the passage through this life, all who live now, all that will be born after us, all constitute the one body of Christ, while they are each individually members of Christ. (*S* 314.11)

The line in this sermon, "as long as people beget and are begotten, any of the just who make the passage through this life," resonates with *Letter* 102's reference to "all those from the beginning of human race who believed in him and understood him somehow or other, and lived pious and just lives . . ., whenever and wherever they lived; [such persons] were undoubtedly saved through him" (*L* 102.12). Our faith in Christ is the reason we reach out to all others in encounter and dialogue, for we believe that Christ is the revelation of universal divine love, an infinite love that embraces all persons and all creation.

***Dialogue Amidst Religious Division and Persecution.*** Even as I write these words, I am mindful of my Nigerian brothers and sisters, especially the Augustinian friars in northern Nigeria, who live amidst a conflicted Muslim population. Seeking dialogue, remaining open, and listening to those who actively persecute your community is very difficult, as it was for Augustine with regard to extremists in the Donatist sect. The fanatical Boko Haram movement, in Nigeria, that aggressively kidnaps, persecutes, and murders Christians does not represent authentic Islam. Yet their violence has made interreligious dialogue between Christians and Muslims in Nigeria almost impossible. I end with the story of a Nigerian friar by the name of Hilary.

When he was a student at the Augustinian seminary in northern Nigeria, Hilary was among his brothers when a mob, agitated by Boko Haram, attacked their small monastery. The mob threatened them with machetes and, in fact, slashed his head, causing significant injury. Hilary recovered, but admitted that he struggled with feelings of anger and hatred toward Muslim people. For many years, he bore both the physical and the psychological scars of this violence.

His story reminds us that spirituality must take sin into account. With his reflections on original sin, pride, ignorance, and weakness of will, Augustine warns us that we must contend with evil in its various manifestations. Christ continues to suffer in his members afflicted by all kinds of violence and injustice. How to move forward in hope amidst daily persecution, violence, and devastation caused by human pride and its impulse to domination? How do we relate to those whose ignorance and violence render them dangerous actors, either across religious difference or sometimes even within the same religion? We can repeat the challenge Augustine gave in a homily on the First Letter of Saint John:

> Ask God that you may love one another. You should love all people, even your enemies, not because they are your brother or sister, but so that they may become your brother or sister, so that you may always be aflame with such love . . . (*Hom 1 Jn* 10.7)

Or we can again quote Augustine's letter to Proba, who herself had just fled extensive violence in the sack of Rome. "There is no one in the human race to whom we do not owe love, even if not out of mutual love, at least on account of our sharing in a common nature" (*L* 130.6.13).

These words of Augustine, along with Jesus' injunction in the Sermon on the Mount to "do good to those who persecute you" (Matthew 5:44), are hard sayings. But back to Hilary's story. A few years after his encounter with the mob, Father Hilary was assigned to the small Augustinian monastery in Annaba, Algeria, the present-day site of the ancient North African city of Hippo, where Augustine was bishop. It was a difficult assignment for him for obvious reasons. How to live in a Muslim country when one is struggling with the memory of violence on one's person? One day, Hilary was waiting at a traffic light in Annaba to cross the street. Next to him was a Muslim family: mother, father, and their small daughter. To her right, the little girl was holding her mother's hand. To the left stood Hilary. When the crosswalk signal turned green, she looked up at him, smiled, reached out, and took his hand in hers. They safely crossed the road, the little girl protected by her mother on one side and Hilary on the other, a momentarily extended family.

"It touched my heart," Hilary told me. "All my feelings of hatred and resentment melted in that moment of grace." Grace, God's freely given, infinite love for each of us and all of us, comes upon us when we least expect it, from quarters we never suspect, in ways we never imagine. For Augustine in the garden at Milan, it was a mystical child singing, "Take and read." For Hilary at a crosswalk in Hippo, it was a Muslim child asking, "Take my hand." Hold my hand so we can cross safely. Hilary's Augustinian formation helped him recognize this gesture as a moment of grace, as "nothing other than a divine command," as the hand of providence reaching out to him through her little hand to heal "the intense bitterness of my broken heart" (*Conf* IX.12.29).

Augustinian spirituality is a call to live together in the light of God's grace, revealed and confirmed in Christ. It is a call to contemplate that grace in the quiet of the inner cloister of our soul, in the midst of those whose love sustains us, who are the Body of Christ today, the Whole Christ extended throughout time and space. We look forward to the concord of all things in Christ, who "brings unity to all things in heaven and on earth" and "whom God appointed to be head over everything for the church, which is his body, the fullness of him who fills everything in every way" (Ephesians 1:10, 22-23).

The words of Augustine at the end of *Confessions* apply to our spiritual life as it relates to other Catholics, other Christians, members of other religions, and all persons, and indeed to all creation. "All these things we see to be exceedingly good, because you see them in us, you who have given us the Spirit to enable us to see them, and in them to love you" (*Conf* XIII.34.49).

# Prayer

O Lord my God, my one hope,
Listen to me lest out of weariness
I should stop wanting to seek you,
but let me seek your face always, and with ardor.
May you give yourself to me the strength to seek
having caused yourself to be found
and having given me the hope of finding you more and more.
Before you lies my strength and my weakness;
preserve the one, heal the other.
Before you lies my knowledge and my ignorance;
where you have opened to me, receive me as I come in;
where you have shut to me, open to me as I knock.
Let me remember you,
let me understand you,
let me love you.
Increase these things in me
until you refashion me entirely.

*The Trinity* XV.6.51

Domine Deus meus, una spes mea,
exaudi me, ne fatigatus nolim te quaerere,
sed quaeram faciem tuam semper ardenter.
Tu da quaerendi vires,
qui inveniri te fecisti,
et magis magisque inveniendi te spem dedisti.
Coram te est firmitas et infirmitas mea:
illam serva, istam sana.
Coram te est scientia et ignorantia mea:

ubi mihi aperuisti, suscipe intrantem;
ubi clausisti, aperi pulsanti.
Meminerim tui,
intellegam te,
diligam te.
Auge in me ista,
donec me reformes ad integrum.

# Afterword

There is a charming legend about Saint Augustine walking along the seashore, pondering the mystery of God. He was meditating on the Christian teaching of the Trinity. A little child, playing in the sand, distracted him. The child was walking back and forth from the water's edge to a hole dug in the sand. As Augustine approached, he saw that the child had a seashell for scooping up water from the sea. The little one carefully carried the shell brimming with water to pour the contents into the hole. Then back to the sea for more water to repeat the process over and over again.

"What are you doing?" asked Augustine. The child replied, "I'm going to empty the sea into the hole I dug in the sand." "That's impossible," said Augustine. "The sea is far too big to fit into that little hole." The child looked up at Augustine and said, "And you will never be able to fit the infinity of God within the confines of your mind." An angelic message.

The story reminds us of the limits of our words and concepts when it comes to talking about God. A trained rhetorician, Augustine was careful and cautious about using words to speak of God. "So what are we to say about God? If you have fully grasped what you want to say, it isn't God. . . . you have comprehended something else instead of God" (*S* 52.16). "Let us rather make a devout confession of ignorance, instead of a brash profession of knowledge. Certainly it is great bliss to have a little touch or taste of God with the mind, but completely to grasp him, to comprehend him, is altogether impossible" (*S* 117.5).

However, if we believe that we are created in God's image, it seems reasonable that we should be able to talk about God at least to some extent, to get "a little touch or taste" of the divine. "Let the mind worship the uncreated God, by whom it was created with a capacity for him and able to share in him" (*Trin* XIV.4.15). We have a capacity for the spiritual life, but our language and thought are limited when it comes to talking or writing about it.

Writing about Augustinian spirituality is a work of humility. You must begin and carry on all the while making a "devout confession of ignorance," admitting that the words will never grasp the mystery, never comprehend the God they name, never adequately express our experience of God. You have to empty yourself, open yourself, and in a certain sense become obedient to the topic—obedient in the Latin etymology of the word: to *ob-audire* to listen carefully. To listen carefully to what Augustine says when he tries to describe his experience of God, his encounter with Christ, and his love for others. Humility reminds us of the difference between words and the mysteries to which they point, between our words and *the Word*, between sacraments and what stirs beneath them. Humility counsels silence amidst our encounters with the mystery of God.

In the little hill-town of Genazzano, Italy, there is the parish church of Our Mother of Good Counsel. The Augustinian friars have served this parish since the fourteenth century. The story goes that when renovating and enlarging the church, the friars and townspeople witnessed an event they came to consider miraculous. On April 25, 1467, as a wall was being repaired, a marble figure of the Madonna had to be removed. Where the statute had been, there was now an image of Mary and the Child Jesus. It had the appearance of an icon, the kind found in Eastern Christian churches. In fact, it resembled a particular icon venerated by the Christians in Albania, which was under violent siege at that time. Legend has it that the icon escaped from a church in Albania and floated across the Adriatic Sea to Genazzano. The Augustinians and the townspeople gratefully accepted the icon and gave it the name of their parish: Our Mother of Good Counsel.

The "appearance" of the icon and the witness of Albanians as to its origin have made the church in Genazzano a place of pilgrimage and prayer ever since. Many popes, saints, and innumerable ordinary folk have visited the church to pray before the icon of Our Mother of Good Counsel on special occasions or for special intentions. Pope John XXIII visited Genazzano and prayed before the icon on the eve of the Second Vatican Council. It was the site of Augustinian Pope Leo's first visit outside Rome after his election.

Icons are silent. They communicate spiritual meaning through the intricate symbolism of the lines, colors, and calligraphy of their composition. Iconography, the painting or "writing" of an icon, is a deeply contemplative process, done in prayerful silence. And the icon itself remains silent. For seven centuries, Mary and the Child Jesus have been gazing silently, lovingly at pilgrims, great and small, who have visited Genazzano. Not a word all the while. No Marian message, announcement, or warning. Only "the sound of sheer silence." Only those mysterious eyes, silent portals into the divine mystery behind and within their gaze. So we end with Mary's good counsel for all those who seek to live an Augustinian spiritual life. "God speaks in secret, he speaks to many in their hearts; and great is the sound in the great silence of the heart" (*Ex Ps* 38.20).

*Enkindling the Spirit of Unity*

The New City Press book you are holding in your hands is one of the many resources produced by Focolare Media, which is a ministry of the Focolare Movement in North America. The Focolare is a worldwide community of people who feel called to bring about the realization of Jesus' prayer: "That all may be one" (see John 17:21).

Focolare Media wants to be your primary resource for connecting with people, ideas, and practices that build unity. Our mission is to provide content that empowers people to grow spiritually, improve relationships, engage in dialogue, and foster collaboration within the Church and throughout society.

Visit www.focolaremedia.com to learn more about all of New City Press's books, our award-winning magazine *Living City*, videos, podcasts, events, and free resources.